The complete illustrated autobiog
CELEBRATING 50 YEARS OF F

Kevin
SHEEDY

Published by Affirm Press in 2017
28 Thistlethwaite Street, South Melbourne, VIC 3205.
www.affirmpress.com.au
10 9 8 7 6 5 4 3 2 1

National Library of Australia Cataloguing-in-Publication entry available for
this title at www.nla.gov.au

Title: Kevin Sheedy / Kevin Sheedy, author.
ISBN: 9781925584431

Cover and book design by Karen Wallis, Taloula Press
Jacket image: Fairfax Media
Case image: Essendon Football Club
Printed in China by C&C Printing

The complete illustrated autobiography
CELEBRATING 50 YEARS OF FOOTY

Kevin

SHEEDY

CONTENTS

You should always honour your champions and their great moments. That's why we set up our own Hall of Fame at Essendon. I feel lucky to be a part of it.

WHEN YOU'RE ABOUT TO TURN 70 – AND HAVE clocked more than 50 years in senior football – photographs can be the most reliable memories. There are more than 50,000 photos on my iPad, but only a handful are of me. We've had a lot of fun selecting images for this book, ranging from visual reminders of my childhood right through to memorable moments with my grandchildren, Charlotte, Oliver and Tom. (My grandson is the third very significant 'Tom' in my life, joining my dad, Tom Sheedy, and my old coach Tom Hafey, the single biggest influence on my time in football.)

Between the grainy black-and-white photos of my childhood and the coloured digital ones of my grandkids, there has been something called my life – so far. A lot of the pictures have been taken by others, mostly professionals like my schoolfriend Peter Ward. They capture moments at Punt Road, Windy Hill, the 'G and Spotless Stadium, moving as our game progressed from the suburbs of Melbourne to across the nation, and most recently to India. Seventy years ago, who would have thought Aussie Rules would make it so far?

I apologise in advance for how often the words 'I' and 'me' are used in this book, when the truth is every step has been a team effort, but it has stirred up many marvellous memories. It might stir up a lot of yours too, because you will see bits of Australia at different stages in its development, and in the development of your own life. We've come a long way as a country during my threescore and ten, and it's been a wonderful journey for me so far, one I'm delighted to share with you now.

A very different MCG in a very different Melbourne. At school I could look out the window and see the new stands being built for the 1956 Olympics. I hoped I'd get a chance to compete there one day, in whatever sport would take me.

1

ORIGINS

Family shapes us – so does playing footy with a scrunched-up piece of paper. I came from a place of firm support with family and friends. But more important than where you come from is which way you're heading and the opportunity to think big.

THE SHEEDY HERITAGE

IT WILL PROBABLY COME AS NO SURPRISE TO those who thought I was a bit of an outlaw in my playing days that my family history has a link to Ned Kelly. As a boy, my maternal great-grandfather, Michael Cusack, was catching water rats down by Faithfulls Creek just outside Euroa in central Victoria, when he witnessed history. Ned and his gang were using a nearby farm as their base, and they rode right past young Michael on their way to holding up the National Bank and getting away with £2000 in notes, gold and silver. The family probably didn't mention this much at the time, though we've been making up for it ever since!

The other side of our family tree branched into Australia through my grandfather Austin Sheedy. He came out from County Clare in Ireland around 1896 and moved to Yarrawonga near the New South Wales–Victoria border. His first wife was Hannah, the daughter of the owner of a farm on which he found work. When she died he married her first cousin Ellen Manning from County Cork. Tom, my father, was a result of that second marriage. When Austin died, Dad moved with his mum to Melbourne.

The Sheedys ended up living in Moonee Ponds and barracked for Essendon, but the family wasn't involved in the game at this stage (that didn't come until much later, through myself and my brother Pat when we moved to South Yarra). Dad was more interested in what time Tulloch was running on a Saturday afternoon than how many goals John Coleman was kicking. My mum, Irene, also loved the horses, and she got as much pleasure out of Bel Esprit, the champion stallion I have a part-share in, as she did any of my grand finals.

Tom Sheedy and Irene Nixon were married on 11 September 1943 and, being good Catholics, quickly embarked on having a big family. I came along as number three, born on Christmas Eve, 1947. I was lucky that Barbara and Pat came before me, because they did a lot of the caring and sharing in our household and were great influences on me and my younger siblings, Kathleen, Bernard, John and Anne-Maree.

Here's my dad, Thomas Edward Sheedy. He's in his thirties here, before I knew him, and he died at 50. He was a typical Irish Catholic brought up by a hard-nosed family. There was no room for anything beyond work and sport. He was a strict disciplinarian; if you weren't in the first three rows at church, you weren't there early enough. That drove us mad, but we were always there early enough. I got my work ethic from him: he worked nearly every day of his life with just two weeks off a year (thank God for unions because we now have four). Supporting seven kids was a big effort, especially in those days.

DREAMING ABOUT SPORT

WHEN PATRICK AND I FIRST PLAYED FOOTY AS kids it was often with a ball made from paper, which was pretty much all we had. If we got lucky we might play with a tennis ball, and we'd use anything for goals. Sometimes it was the door to the outside dunny – isn't that a great Australian word? – or maybe a couple of trees, or some bins. You didn't need much to have a game, and I guess that's how I got hooked.

I could have been a fisherman after spending so much time trying to catch redfin in the Ornamental Lake in Melbourne's Botanic Gardens. It's a place I still love to visit now, particularly in autumn when the leaves are green and gold: Australia's colours. Maybe that's where my love of Australia started – about the same time all those famous Australian names were winning gold medals at the 1956 Olympics. From my classroom, I could watch the new stands for those Games being built in the Melbourne Cricket Ground. It was then I started dreaming that sport might play a big role in my life; why wouldn't you want to be like Betty Cuthbert, Shirley Strickland, Murray Rose, John Devitt, Dawn Fraser and Lorraine Crapp? Where the dreaming starts has always been a major focus for me, particularly when I'm talking to kids.

Football became my choice partly because I couldn't swim that well and was never that quick, and partly because I wasn't too bad at arithmetic. It had to be a team sport to give me a chance of getting a game. I looked at cricket and saw there were 11 in a team but only one leg-spinner, and I couldn't see Richie Benaud, one of my childhood heroes, stepping aside for me.

In football, there were 20 players on a team and 10 clubs in Victoria, so it seemed like a no-brainer. But even with those improved odds, I needed to overcome a significant disadvantage in pace and height. So I tried to focus on skills. Pat was my first skills coach, teaching me how to hold the ball to kick it. The new technology of television became my next coach – not that we had one at home, of course. Television might have arrived with the 1956 Olympics, but myself and Pat and our friends had to watch the games through the shop windows of Chapel Street.

> What I did have, though, thanks to my parents, was a strong work ethic. I knew I'd have to work hard to make it in footy, and applying myself felt like second nature.

I figured out a way to combine work and football when I got a job as a lolly boy at the 1958 Grand Final, when Collingwood, coached by Phonse Kyne, beat Melbourne, coached by Norm Smith. Another job that

This is the first photo I can actually remember – possibly because I was petrified, although I look pretty happy. There's my father in the background, how I remember him. Mums were always in the foreground, taking care, while dads were a shadow looking on from afar.

All the family at the Royal Botanic Gardens: Mum and Dad and the seven brothers and sisters. Dad loved the Botanic Gardens, and that rubbed off on me; I spend more time there than anywhere else. The coffee shop in the gardens was my meeting place when I was at Richmond. Keep close to nature and you won't go wrong.

The Euroa premiership team 1922. My great grandfather Michael Cusack is the goal umpire with the flags in the middle of the back row, and Michael's son Tom was the boundary umpire – a pair of 'Martians' in my own family! Croke Park in Dublin, where we took the International Rules team in 2006, has a Cusack stand. I don't think they were related, but I still stood in front of it for good luck.

helped with football was my paper round, which involved jumping on and off trams to sell papers to people coming home from work. That really helped sharpen my sense of timing; trust me, a tram could be even tougher than Leigh Matthews if you ran into one.

I left school early, deciding to begin an apprenticeship as a plumber. Plumbers work hard, digging ditches and standing in mud and other brown stuff – for me it was a means to an end. What I really wanted to do was play football, but I knew the only way through was to work harder and smarter than all the players who were more naturally gifted. As Ned Kelly found out, you can only get away with robbing banks for so long.

South Yarra in the 1950s. Not a lot going on. Tin shed in the back, and my brother Patrick and sister Barbara on either side. Still another four siblings to go.

Paper rounds and paper balls

As my brother makes a living these days on the public speaking circuit, you might not believe that when he was a little boy Kevin was the quiet one. I was the yapper and Kevin was more of the observer, something he still does now when he's not talking.

I am around a year and a quarter older than Kevin, which is, apart from Anne-Marie, how the seven siblings were spaced out. (Anne-Marie is 15 years younger than me.) Kevin and I did a lot of things together, including backyard football where there was no give and take. The ball was made from paper because our family couldn't afford a real one, and anyway, Mum and Dad were more into the races than football.

Every year Dad would take us to the Newmarket sales even though he could never afford to buy a horse. I think he wanted to buy Phar Lap for fifty pounds. He'd get the catalogue and wander around the stables looking at horses, dragging us behind him. He had this big old overcoat that he wore everywhere, and when we'd come home from the sales without a horse, Mum would say, 'I don't know why you bother going to the sales, Tom. You only ever come home with fleas.'

Mum loved the races, too. Every year she'd go to the Warrnambool Carnival, and when she died they asked Kevin to come down the next year to be the Ambassador for the Carnival. Being Kevin, he did a great job. He got to stay in the same motel that Mum stayed in every year. He rang to ask me which room was Mum's but he didn't know that they had renovated the place and turned the little room that

Mum stayed in into an en suite for the bigger room. So I said, 'When you go into the bathroom be careful what you get up to – Mum will be watching.' As part of the renovation, they had even painted the room black and red.

Dad was a tough bloke. He'd only tell you once to do something and if you didn't, you were in trouble. He worked hard to put food on the table for us, but sadly, he never got to see the fruits of his labour, how his family turned out, because he got motor neurone disease and died in 1966. It was just after Dad's death that Kevin began to get really close to Tom Hafey.

Because there was no spare money, Kevin and I both had paper rounds with Mr Moller's newsagency on Commercial Road, Prahran, to help with the family finances. He was kind-hearted, Mr Moller, but he was tight about the money, and if you were short, you had to make it up out of your own pocket. We had a few tricks to make sure we made extra money of our own. If someone gave you sixpence and the tram was about to go, or the lights were turning green, you'd shovel around in your bag pretending to be looking for the threepence change and time would beat them. It was probably me who taught Kevin how to do that. Another thing we learned was that if Richmond or Collingwood won, we sold a lot more papers than if it was Essendon or some of the other teams that were further away from Prahran and South Yarra, which is probably why I still barrack for Collingwood now.

Kevin and I got into football a lot more when we went to school at St Ignatius on the hill and discovered team sports. You went in hard, but you also had to make sure not to damage your clothes. We only ever got new uniforms once a year, and if you put a hole in your pants, that's how it stayed. Kevin was never a great kick and didn't take a lot of marks, but like Kevin Bartlett, who used to help us with our paper rounds even though he didn't have one of his own, he was very good at reading the packs. And while he was never that fast, he knew how to get from A to C by cutting out B. But the thing that you really noticed about him was how determined he always was.

After St Ignatius I went to De La Salle, but Kevin went to St Joseph's; I don't think Mum and Dad could afford both of us going to De La Salle. After St Joseph's Kevin went to Prahran Technical College to learn a trade. Kevin played a lot of football with Try Boys but it wasn't until he got to Prahran that he really clicked, and we all know the rest: 251 games for Richmond. He had a lot of crap in him as a player; he'd start blues, but keep on playing sensible football while his opponents were running around trying to whack him back.

Mum became a Richmond supporter and she enjoyed everything about Kevin's career as a player, then as a coach with Essendon. The only thing she didn't like was when he did that slitting of the throat thing to Mitchell White from the West Coast. Getting the gig at Essendon was the love of his life. When he went for the job he knew more about the Bombers than they realised because he had been following them all his life and would often go to Windy Hill with Mr Moller to watch them play.

What sort of a brother is Kevin Sheedy? Well we think of him as everyone's brother. Because of all the demands on him, even now he's often away from home, but he knows where I am and I know where he is. They say you can't choose your rellies but he's been a bonzer bloke to watch. They will build a statue to him in 20 years and he'll be happy to have a pigeon shit on him.

Patrick Sheedy, Kevin's brother.

BEST AND FAIREST

WOMEN HAVE LONG BEEN A LIFELINE OF OUR GAME, since way before the AFL Women's competition. For myself, two women were instrumental in getting me into the game, and I dare say I owe to them a fair chunk of the 50 years I've worked in footy.

The first was Sister Rupert. She came from County Clare and had a thick Irish brogue that was not always easy to understand. She would probably have said the same about our Aussie accents, and she certainly didn't understand the game we called Aussie Rules.

What she knew for sure, though, was that when you want a class full of young boys to sit quietly and concentrate, you have to wear them out first. She'd take us off to Fawkner Park in South Yarra (because the school grounds were not big enough) and divide us up and into teams of about nine or ten – a kind of ecclesiastical version of football.

Now, there might be four of these games going on across the same pitch, so spatial awareness was essential. The challenge was watching the ball and your man, all while trying not to get cleaned up by someone from another game watching a different ball and a different man. In that sense Sister Rupert was a very innovative coach. She also learned to love the game and told us that watching it on the television was the only time she stayed up after 9pm. I used to love those games in Fawkner Park, playing with abandon for pure love of the contest.

Veronica Nolan was the next influential woman in my footy life. A team of us from St Joseph's School were let loose in Toorak Park for a football tournament. We were straining at the leash and ready to play, but we lacked the vital ingredient of a coach. So the job went to Veronica, the elder sister of a couple of the boys in the team. She did a great job of organising us and ended up coaching the team for two years. Once word got out beyond South Yarra, she was even interviewed for *The Sun* newspaper.

At the beginning our jumpers were old and scraggy, and there weren't enough to go around. So Veronica's mother raised money to buy new ones, and at the end of every game she'd take them home and wash them herself because she thought – probably quite rightly – that we couldn't be trusted to bring them back. They were local heroes for me.

Having women working in football has always seemed like the most natural thing in the world to me, which was one of the reasons I was so happy to get behind the Essendon Women's Network, supporting the women of Essendon and raising funds for the club, with Joan Kirner, Linda Dessau, Di Gribble, Joanne Albert and Jane Clifton. I was equally pleased to work with Carolyn Brown on the book *Football's Women: the Forgotten Heroes*. All the Sister Ruperts and Veronica Nolans needed to be recognised for what they have done for the game. 🏉

Of all the incredible women who shaped my early years, my mum has to be the biggest influence of all.

ABOVE: A fun shot at home. Mum was very encouraging of my football interests and let me paint my room black and gold in our house in Armadale. The people who bought the house from her must have thought it was a shrine by some mad kid. They probably painted over it straight away.

RIGHT: The toughest woman I met: loyal, great worker and very headstrong. Mum was also a good recruitment agent, a ruthless but excellent judge of men. If she didn't like a person you were knocking around with, she'd say, 'Just be aware.' That would ring alarm bells for me.

TRY BOYS AND TWO BLUES

AFTER I LEFT SCHOOL, THE FIRST REAL STEP IN my football career was Try Boys. Try Boys was a charity set up in the 1880s by William Mark Forster, a wealthy Melbourne businessman who wanted to keep young boys out of trouble. Little did he know that Try Boys in Cromwell Road, South Yarra would let 'trouble' straight onto the team: Kevin Bartlett.

Around that time, thanks to Bill Maxwell, who was a science and maths teacher at Prahran Technical College, I got a trial with Melbourne Football Club – along with about 100 other young hopefuls. I cleaned my boots, combed my hair and did my best to look like a footballer worthy of Melbourne, the club of the establishment. But the establishment said, 'no thanks' to the teenager from South Yarra, so other options had to be explored.

At 16, I was too old to go back to Try Boys, so I thought I might as well try the Prahran Under 19s in the old Victorian Football Association. Boy, wasn't that a lesson – playing against blokes who were two and three years older than me and already drove cars and motorbikes.

The manager of Prahran – and my first ever manager in football – was Jack Morgans, a true blue Two Blue if ever there was one. He's 90 now, and in that time there isn't a job he hasn't done for Prahran footy club.

He saw us through to a premiership in 1966, and was at the heart of our 50th anniversary celebration in 2016. Up until Prahran, the backline had been my home, but the Two Blues gave me opportunities at half-forward and in the centre.

By this time in my life the value of an opportunity was becoming very clear to me. You had to take it with all the energy you could find. You'd watch, you'd listen, you'd train, and when it came to Sunday (when VFA games were played) you'd give it everything you could and just hope that somewhere in the crowd there might be someone from a VFL club who had heard how dedicated you were and come down to have a look for themselves.

Thankfully there was. They were from the club whose zone we had lived in since my parents moved from South Yarra to Armadale: it was called Richmond. 🏈

1981, celebrating Kevin Bartlett's 350th game with some Richmond legends: (from left) Graeme Bond, me, Mike Green, Tom Hafey, Mervyn Keane and Francis Bourke.

Irrepressible force

Kevin Sheedy celebrates 50 years in VFL/AFL football in 2017; what a journey it has been, and it's not over yet. I might be biased but I believe no one in the history of the game has made a greater contribution to Australian Rules Football: a champion player, a three-time premiership star for Richmond and a legendary four-time premiership coach of Essendon, and a visionary who championed Indigenous players and was the driving force behind Anzac Day and Dreamtime games at the MCG.

And when the AFL wanted to win the hearts of fans and to spread the gospel of the game he loves, there was only one person who could sell the game in Greater Western Sydney, and that was Sheeds. As the inaugural coach of the Giants he set the club up to be a juggernaut of the competition for now and into the future. I'm not surprised by any of his achievements for I have known Kevin as a friend for 60 years. As ten-year-olds we played footy in the local park in South Yarra after school, pretending to be our idols. Sheeds barracked for Essendon and I loved Footscray. We went to the same school, Prahran Technical College, and played for the same junior football team, Try Boys Society.

How lucky have I been to have had a front row seat in witnessing the sporting journey that makes Sheeds arguably the best-known football personality in the country? He is a great role model who, from humble beginnings, followed his dream of being a footballer. That's all he wanted to be as a kid. Selling papers in and around South Yarra, a suburb that had pubs on every corner, he was known as the paper boy who would wear his number 10 Essendon jumper to sell papers at the six o'clock swill. Who wouldn't buy a paper on a Saturday night from a young boy supporting his team, win, lose or draw? It showed the early mind of a street-smart kid who would never take no for an answer.

He was rejected by the Melbourne footy club for he was never an outstanding junior player, and as the powerhouse club of the competition back then the Demons could be fussy. Sheeds was not a prodigious kick, nor was he quick of foot, but what was not recognised by the Dees was that he was quick of mind and he was driven.

Prahran footy club gave him his senior start and I was thrilled when my mate was recruited to Tigerland in 1967. The VFA refused to give Sheeds a clearance but he followed his dream and backed himself to make it in the big time. Some would say at the time it was a silly move, as Richmond already had the best centreman in the game in the great Billy Barrot, who was a booming kick, agile, explosive, a strong mark and a match winner.

Sheeds at that time possessed none of those qualities. He was regarded as slow and less than an adequate kick with a bit of lair about his game, but at the same time a ball magnet. It didn't take Sheeds long to lock horns with Barrot, and soon they were throwing punches at each other at training. Kevin injured his knee in 1967, the year Richmond won the premiership for the first time in 23 years, and it must have been heartbreaking for him to watch from the sidelines.

Sheeds, though, had a fan in legendary Richmond coach Tom Hafey, who was a back-pocket player of limited ability for the Tigers, and who had read about his own sacking as a player in the paper without warning. He admired Kevin's persistence and work ethic. Tommy, I suspect, saw a lot of himself in Sheeds and found him a new position in the back pocket. What a thrill it was for me to have my childhood friend as a premiership player when we won the 1969 flag defeating Carlton. Flags followed in 1973 and 1974, and Hafey forever claimed that Sheeds was the greatest back-pocket player to have ever played the game.

When Kevin retired during the 1979 season after being captain the year before, he stayed on at the club as a skills coach. I had been banished from rover to the half-forward flank, and Sheeds worked tirelessly on my kicking skills so I could make the best of my opportunities as a small forward. My old mate extended my career by another four years and played a major role in me playing in another premiership in 1980. He would say that's what friends are for.

I am so proud of Kevin Sheedy and all he has achieved, and count myself lucky that I have known him for most of my life. What a story it has been, and it's not over yet!

Kevin Bartlett AM, Richmond premiership player and AFL Hall of Fame Legend.

The tortoise and the hare. Even though we changed clubs, we never separated. Great friends forever.

ROGERS

Kellogg's ★ KEVIN SHEEDY

It's interesting how people see you when they do caricatures – big nose, red nose, fat face – but some are fantastic. I often think about the significance of art in the history of footy. On statues, for example, it's important how the artist projects the person to the public. The statue of Kevin Bartlett outside the MCG is a ripper.

2

THE YELLOW & BLACK

Richmond became like an extension of my family, and they made me feel welcome straight away. It was just as well because if it didn't work out with the Tigers I would have been banned from playing football anywhere for the next five years.

FROM CUB TO TIGER

THE LETTER INVITING ME TO PLAY FOR THE Richmond Football Club is one of the most beautiful things I have ever seen. It talked about my performances for Prahran – so they *had* been watching – and informed me that as I was now living in the club's recruitment zone I could become a Richmond player 'if I wished to'. How about more than anything on earth? There was something else special about that letter: it had Richmond on the top of the page and Richmond on the bottom, because it was signed by Graeme Richmond, the General Manager, and a man who would become one of the biggest influences on my life.

But first I had to find my way out of a massive stoush between the Victorian Football League (VFL) and the Victorian Football Association (VFA). Back in the 1960s they were savage on each other, and as a result of their disagreement I had to transfer to the VFL without clearance, which meant I was banned by the VFA from playing football anywhere in Australia for five years – akin to a life sentence. It was Richmond or bust for me. Mum said, 'If you believe in yourself, then go.' You should always listen to your mum.

Richmond made me feel welcome from the outset (and Sister Rupert started supporting them when I joined – she later followed me to Essendon, bless her). It's one of the things that has remained with me ever since, how important that first meeting is for all the young players – and their families – who you bring into your club.

In 1967, 50 years ago, I played my first senior game for the Tigers – and I hadn't even played in the reserves yet. Right from that first game I was number 10, the number of my childhood hero, Essendon's Ian 'Bluey' Shelton. I still have all the telegrams that were sent to me that day. They were from former customers on my paper round, Joan, Phil, Cheryl and Buster; one from Tom Hafey's brother Peter; my old plumbing bosses Brian and Maria Wishart; Prahran teammates and board people. It was a massive occasion for me, not least because I'd crossed without a clearance. Knowing I had the support of these people behind me was great.

I found myself on a steep learning curve in that first game, facing up against the likes of Daryl Peoples from Fitzroy and Geelong's team of the century superstar Denis Marshall – it was on the wing too, and I was probably a bit too slow for that position. But I did okay and soon got my first game in the reserves. 🏉

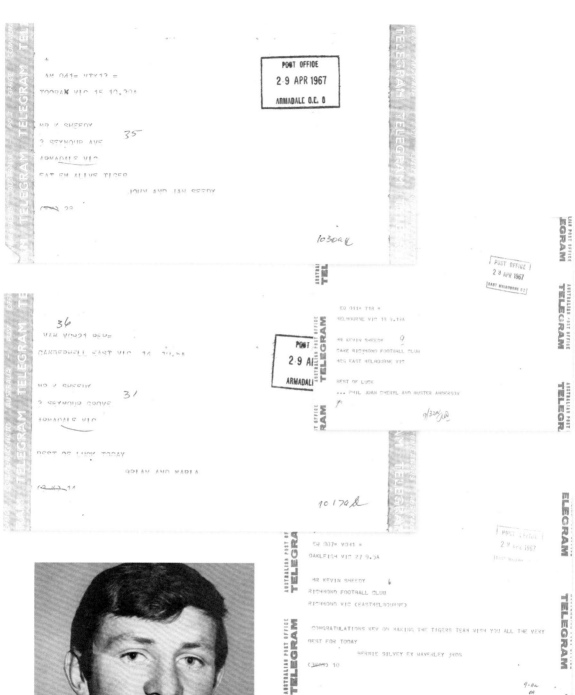

ABOVE: *Telegrams of encouragement from friends and family on the day of my first game for Richmond.*

LEFT: *The worst marshmallow photo I've ever had. How soft does he look? I toughened up a bit.*

Kevin Sheedy in his Richmond days ... barracked for Essendon as a boy

THE RICHMOND WAY

ALMOST AS SOON AS MY CAREER BEGAN WITH Richmond, I got a serious knee injury, which put it in even more jeopardy than the VFA had. It meant watching Richmond's first premiership in 24 years from the stands, while at the same time doing everything I could to make sure of a full recovery.

The Melbourne champion John Townsend had the same injury and was one of the first people to make a successful recovery. Though he wouldn't have known it, I followed him everywhere, watching everything he did. I also got constant encouragement and reassurance from my coach, Tom Hafey. It's easy to look back now, after three premierships, but back then I didn't know if I'd ever play another game, so Tom's words meant a lot to me.

People don't give Tom Hafey enough credit for the way he moved players around to get the best out of them in matches and in their careers; in three grand finals he played Barry 'Bones' Richardson at half-forward, fullback and full-forward. I always thought it was funny that Barry, who was a physiotherapist, was called Bones – shouldn't it have been Muscles? By the time I was fit again in 1968, Tommy – who had a brilliant centreman in the electrifying Billy Barrot, and so didn't need me there – had decided on me as good back pocket. By the 1969 season, my recovery and my performances down back were good enough for a regular spot in the seniors. Still, I was always aware that the next game could be my last if I didn't do everything that Tom Hafey and Graeme Richmond expected from a short, slow back pocket. So yeah, a few blokes got hit hard.

The reward was one of the great moments of my life: winning the 1969 premiership in front of 120,000 people at the MCG, the ground I had first dreamed about playing on when I was sitting in my classroom. Dreams really do come true, if you work hard enough.

Ron Barassi, the Carlton coach, said the Blues lost because his champion forwards – Alex Jesaulenko, Robert Walls, Brent Crosswell and Syd Jackson – all had a bad day. Another view might be that the Richmond blokes down back, including the number 10, had a good day. 🏉

TOP LEFT: Technique was everything, and I studied all different sports to improve mine. Most players today don't have great technique, missing handballs 8 metres away that they shouldn't. I'm not criticising them for missing handballs under pressure, but if you break your teammate's stride then that's poor technique.

TOP RIGHT: Your parents gave you a name, so write the autograph properly. Thank you, Sister Rupert.

BOTTOM: I had to learn to kick properly, and because I always had tight hamstrings I had to make sure I got the leg to follow through perfectly. Not necessarily Bernie Quinlan. 1974.

DRAFTED

THANKS TO A DRAFT CONCEIVED BY SIR ROBERT Menzies, on the Monday following my first ever premiership I began my two years of national service in the army. It was a big lesson in perspective: in two days I went from runner-up Best and Fairest in the VFL, and all the pomp that goes with it, to peeling potatoes as a bottom-ranked private. Conscription knocked around the careers of many others, like the Australian cricketer Dougie Walters and King of Pop Normie Rowe, but for me it was a huge plus, not only for the life lessons, but because it was where I first started to think I might able to become a coach.

Major Arthur Fittock (now Major-General), the head of 21 Construction Squadron at Puckapunyal – the Victorian base also known as Pucka-bloody-punyal – asked me to coach the unit's Australian Rules team. Tommy Hafey could give a good spray at Richmond – 'You're nothing but a back-pocket plumber, Kevin, and don't you forget it!' – but you had to choose your words carefully when giving a spray to someone who was your superior (there were an awful lot of spuds that needed peeling at Pucka-bloody-punyal). Also, you didn't want to tell someone to go out there and show a bit of courage when they were just back from showing real courage in Vietnam.

Major Fittock also taught me the importance of getting everything in place before going into action. It was something that particularly came back to me at Greater Western Sydney. We were part of an invasion and the forces of resistance were everywhere, the NRL and soccer laying out minefields. So, like soldiers landing on a beach, we couldn't afford to make any mistakes.

Back at Richmond, there was another lesson being learned: how politics can ruin a footy club. Amazingly it had nearly happened in 1969 when some people had wanted to sack Tom Hafey – 1969, not even two years after he had won the club its first flag in 24 years. Tom was never a good politician, and that got him in the end. In 1976, when he found out that he didn't have the full support of the board, he quit and went on to take Collingwood to five grand final appearances. How many of those could have been Richmond premierships? That question should haunt the people who drove him out. Certainly, Richmond is haunted by that decision. Four premierships in a decade under Tom – only one since he left. 🏈

I became a gladiator when I played. I always took footy as a gladiatorial game, but I wasn't skilful, and that annoyed a lot of people.

(From left) Myself, Royce Hart, Neil Balme, Bryan Wood and Francis Bourke. I was pretending to have a glass of beer in my hand there because I wouldn't drink. I didn't want to ruin the shot, but neither did I want to promote beer. Tom Hafey was really unimpressed at having a beer sponsorship, but they wanted me in the shot because I was a plumber and that would play well with the punters. I didn't drink till I was 35 or so.

Both of these beers belong to Francis Bourke, five-time premiership player and one of the greatest footballers ever. I imagine I'm gritting my teeth here, 'Do I really have to be in the photo?'

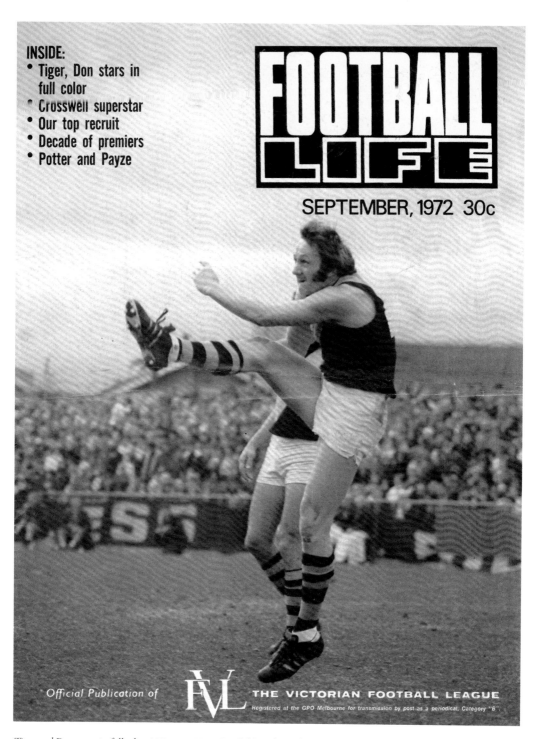

INSIDE:
* Tiger, Don stars in full color
* Crosswell superstar
* Our top recruit
* Decade of premiers
* Potter and Payze

FOOTBALL LIFE

SEPTEMBER, 1972 30c

Official Publication of FVL **THE VICTORIAN FOOTBALL LEAGUE**
Registered at the GPO Melbourne for transmission by post as a periodical, Category "B".

Tiger and Dons stars in full colour! 30 cents, 1972. Geez life has changed.

Sapper Sheedy

I first met Kevin when he literally marched into the 21 Construction Squadron – which I commanded – nearly 50 years ago as a National Serviceman. In the 1960s and 1970s, all young men had to register for national service at the age of 18. The ballot system worked without fear or favour. It didn't matter who you were, if your birthday was drawn out, you became a 'Nasho' and did two years in the Army.

> As a qualified plumber, he was a natural for the engineers. As a VFL premiership player, he qualified for another important role at Puckapunyal. I was a Rugby Union player, and the 21 Construction Squad's Rugby Union team was very successful, but you couldn't say the same for the Aussie Rules team. I was getting a bit cross with them about their lack of success.

Then, late in 1969, I remember the Aussie Rules players coming to me and asking who would be the coach for next year. When I asked them who they thought it should be they said, 'Sapper Sheedy'. I said that there was no one by that name on my books at Puckapunyal, but they told me there soon would be and that he played in the VFL for Richmond.

When this young plumber/footballer arrived, he looked the part in his khaki uniform, chest out and eager to do well. He had a lot of confidence, and the other things I noticed about him were that he quickly won the confidence of others and always seemed to know what to do to get the job done. However, he wasn't all that keen to be part of the Australian Rules team for 21 Construction Squad. Because Puckapunyal was so close to Melbourne, he still wanted to play for Richmond. That would only happen if the Army made it possible, so I proposed a deal: he would get time off to train and play with Richmond if he agreed to coach and play with his army mates. (The deal was no more than I would do for any soldier, but I doubt Kevin knew that at the time.)

Success came quickly. In 1970, 21 Construction Squad won the competition among the other units based at Puckapunyal, and in 1971 they again made the grand final. What happened that day gives a good insight into Kevin Sheedy's character: he had been injured playing for Richmond on the weekend, and the club had asked him not to play mid-week. I told him it was okay if he didn't play, so long as the team won. But they were behind at three-quarter time, and that's when I looked to the huddle and saw Kevin getting into his gear. And yes, 21 Construction Squad won.

Kevin learned a lot about leadership in his time in the Army and he would have learned about diplomacy too because some of the people in his team were his superior officers. If he said something to them on the field or during his half- and quarter-time talks that they didn't like, they could put him on detention. Kevin left the Army a different person to the one who had arrived two years earlier, having gained a lot of insight into what makes a leader and what you must do to get the job done.

Today, those who served with him remember a soldier on whom we could all rely. Those officers, warrant officers, non-commissioned officers and soldiers are proud to have shared a little of his life, and follow his continuing commitments with great enthusiasm. His achievements since he left us at Puckapunyal certainly reflect many of the ideals of the Australian Army.

Major-General Arthur Fittock AO (retired).

Crackers Keenan and me having it out at a hair salon in a Melbourne v Richmond match. I'd always have a go at the big fellas, ably supported here by umpire Mick Dye. Mick never reported me – but then I did select him in my team back in the Army. Mick was a dual premiership player at Puckapunyal, a good little back pocket who you could throw forward knowing he would get you a goal every time. He went on to umpire the 1981 grand final – a pretty good effort.

1969 PREMIERSHIP

THE QUESTION IS ASKED OFTEN, WHICH PREMIERSHIP do you treasure the most? The answer is simple: you love all your children the same, and you love all your premierships the same. The one at Prahran was important, and it was great to have been able to celebrate the 50th anniversary in 2016 with so many of my old teammates. Premierships create lifelong bonds.

Because of the knee injury in 1967, getting back to play in the 1969 Grand Final was a special moment. I vividly remember that day. We'd only just made the finals on percentages, and because Carlton had the week off. We were supposed to run out of legs. But whoever was saying that had never trained under Tommy Hafey. He always had a lot of good ideas to keep us physically and mentally fit.

Tommy would call in fitness guru Percy Cerutty to take training. Cerutty had trained Herb Elliott to an Olympic gold medal, running him up and down the sandhills on the Mornington Peninsula until Herb could run 1500 metres faster than anyone in the world. Between 1957 and 1961, Herb Elliott never lost a race over 1500 metres, including for the gold medal at the 1960 Rome Olympics. Percy's motto – which came to be the name of his biography – was, 'Why die?' Well, many times he nearly bloody well killed us!

Tom was also good at the psychological stuff. He once had Dennis Lillee and Rod Marsh

Wasn't Tom Hafey unbelievable? His fourth year and he'd won two premierships. In between he missed out on the finals with 14 wins.
This was the last year that the crowd was allowed onto the ground – wouldn't you love to know the names of these Tigers fans now?

ABOVE: KB running out for his 400th game, – and one of his last. (It definitely wasn't the 1969 Grand Final because Kevin had hair then.) He was one of the best players I played footy with: five Best and Fairests, five premierships, five handballs (three of them were up against a brick wall at training one night, which leaves two on the field of play).

OPPOSITE: In the boardroom at Tigerland meeting two of Australia's greatest ever Test cricketers, Rod Marsh and Dennis Lillee, after we'd had a kick on Punt Oval. They both played with the spirit of a Tiger, and they could both kick a footy, too. And Barry Richardson, the most unheralded Richmond premiership player. Three premierships in three different positions – sensational effort.

come down to talk to us about discipline and hard work in cricket. Tommy's message was clear: 'I've brought in two people from the best cricket team in the world to talk to you blokes to make sure you become the best Australian Rules footballers in the world.' After the talk, Rod and Dennis put on footy boots and had a kick with Barry Richardson and me. They'd both had a kick as kids growing up in Western Australia, but they were better cricketers than footballers. To me Dennis Lillee was the epitome of everything the successful Australian sportsperson should be. He was dedicated, he was disciplined and he was just the most aggressive competitor you could find. He had also overcome a serious injury to continue his career, something else to respect.

We led by 22 points at half-time in the 1969 Grand Final, but in the third quarter we did look gone, especially when Brent Crosswell found some of the form that Ron Barassi (in retrospect) reckons he lost that day. We had conceded four goals before a trademark piece of individual brilliance from

Brent put the Blues in front by four points at the final break. Billy Barrot set us off in the final quarter, a great mark followed by a goal in the ninth minute. Then it was the Kevin Bartlett show.

Kevin still puts on a great show on the speaking circuit – very clever, very funny. Whenever we do a show together, I end up being Dean Martin to his Jerry Lewis. Remember that famous Jerry Lewis line? 'People hate me because I am a multifaceted, talented, wealthy, internationally famous genius.' Add, 'and I don't handball' and you've got Kevin Bartlett.

When he's in his Jerry Lewis comedian role, Kevin does this great little skit about being worried, very worried, about the future of the game, because there aren't any Kevins playing any more, not one on any AFL team's list in contrast to our playing days when Richmond, and the other clubs, were full of Kevins. But seriously, we both agree that the lack of Kevins is more than compensated for now by names like Bachar, Orazio and Majak.

Mentor and friend

THE NAME TOM HAS PLAYED A BIG PART IN MY LIFE. MY FATHER WAS TOM SHEEDY. WHEN HE DIED, IT was around the same time that I was discovering another Tom: Tommy Hafey, a man who provided me with so much guidance in my life, not just in football.

When Tom Hafey died, I wrote: 'There are many types of love. The love between a husband and wife. The love between a parent and a child. Family love. And there is the special love that joins people who don't share bloodlines, but end up sharing just about everything else along the journey of life. I love Tommy Hafey. He was the Tommy who stepped into my life at the time my father, also called Tom, died when I was still a teenager. He was the Tommy who, as I went through the ups and downs every footballer has early in their career, picked me up when the ball bounced the wrong way and I got clobbered. He was the Tommy who pulled me down when I got ahead of myself. "You're not that good, Kevin. Remember you're just a back-pocket plumber and the world's got plenty of those."'

A decade ago Tommy wrote down some things about me for my memoir, words I cherish now that I can't speak with him in person over a cup of tea and a biscuit:

Whenever I am asked my opinion of Kevin Sheedy my reply is simply, 'he has done everything he could to get the absolute best out of himself'. You can say that about him as a player, as a coach and a person.

I first heard about Kevin Sheedy when I was coach of Richmond. We were told there was a skinny kid down at Prahran who might have a bit of potential as a VFL player. When I got to know Kevin better after he came to the Tigers, I discovered this young bloke with a terrific passion to improve his game. I would not be giving away any secrets if I said that when Kevin came to Punt Road, he had a lot to learn – a real lot! The thing about Kevin that made us decide to persevere with him was his unbelievable eagerness to learn. Kevin is a great talker, but he was also then – and still is now – a great listener.

He realised very early on that football would give him opportunities in life way beyond what his qualifications as a plumber offered. But he knew that would only happen if he worked harder than everyone else.

In many ways, he probably saw me as an example of that. I was hardly the greatest footballer in the history of the game, but I worked hard to get my 67 games with Richmond. Like Kevin, I had a trade to fall back on – printer. However, it was football that was my real passion and which could take me places that printing wouldn't.

When Kevin was injured so early in his time at Richmond, he could have given up. Instead, he went out of his way to make sure that when he got over his knee operation, he would be fitter and stronger than before. He went out and learned as much as he could about the injury, then about

what he needed to do to ensure a proper rehabilitation. That's Kevin – whenever he's confronted with an issue, he learns as much about it as he can. It was the same when he was in the Army. He reckoned that if he was going to be sent to Vietnam, he should know as much as possible about the people he would be fighting against.

I know that when Kevin became a coach he always wanted to do well against me. I am proud that in his early days as a coach he used a lot of the things he had learned from me and others at Richmond.

Some of the people at Richmond reckoned that Kevin took anything that wasn't nailed down from Punt Road to Windy Hill!

As he developed as a coach, though, other clubs were soon taking his ideas, and not just on the field. He is one of the best thinkers about football we have ever seen, and one of the game's greatest promoters, helping the game develop in places as diverse as the Tiwi Islands and Sydney. I don't think Kevin will be satisfied until every town and suburb in Australia has its own Australian footy team.

A cup of tea with Tom Hafey. He was just the best person – legendary. He was my biggest influence in footy and in life, and I would not be the person I am if not for him. We met in 1966, the year before I was recruited by Richmond; he would have been checking me out then – a bloody scary thought.

I note that Kevin and Harry Beitzel take credit for getting me the job as coach of the Sydney Swans in 1985. Thanks, Kevin, it was a wonderful experience for Maureen and me: living close to the beach, having club functions at the Bourbon and Beefsteak in the Cross, trying to educate people about our game. I reckon we did a pretty good job too. I know they really enjoyed the time in 1987 at the Sydney Cricket Ground when we thrashed the Bombers by 163 points. I doubt the national competition would be anywhere near as successful as it is today without the creative input of Kevin Sheedy.

When we were recruiting people to Richmond in the 1960s, Graeme Richmond and I were not just looking for good players; we wanted good people. You want people who are prepared to work hard, stick to the team rules and be really loyal to what you are trying to achieve. That pretty much sums up Kevin in his playing days.

I have known Kevin for more than 40 years. We have worked together closely on any number of projects, we have coached against each other, we have chatted for hours over endless cups of tea. I reckon I know him as well as just about anyone. Kevin Sheedy is a sensational person. And like all of us he keeps getting better with age.

Thanks, Tom. And thanks to my daughter Chelsea I now have a third Tom in my life: my new grandson.

The Peoples Coach

Tommy Hafey's
Finals Record
1966 - 1988 / 23 Years

Year	Event	Venue	Match		Crowd	Result	Margin
1966	MISSES	5th	13 WINS	123%			
1967	2nd SEMI FINAL	MCG	RICH V CAR	ATT	99,051	WIN	40PTS
	GRAND FINAL	MCG	RICH V GEE	ATT	109,396	WIN	9PTS
1968	MISSES	5th	14 WINS	123%			
1969	1st SEMI FINAL	MCG	RICH V GEE	ATT	101,233	WIN	118PTS
	PRE FINAL	MCG	RICH V COLL	ATT	107,279	WIN	26PTS
	GRAND FINAL	MCG	RICH V CAR	ATT	119,165	WIN	25PTS
1970	MISSES	6th	12 WINS	101%	*22 GAMES FIRST YEAR IN V.F.L*		
1971	1st SEMI FINAL	MCG	RICH V COLL	ATT	99,000	WIN	44PTS
	PRE FINAL	MCG	RICH V STK	ATT	102,494	LOSS	30PTS
1972	QUAL FINAL	MCG	RICH V COLL	ATT	91,900	WIN	44PTS
	1st 2nd SEMI	WAV	RICH V CAR	ATT	54,338	DRAW	
	2nd 2nd SEMI	MCG	RICH V CAR	ATT	92,670	WIN	41PTS
	GRAND FINAL	MCG	RICH V CAR	ATT	112,393	LOSS	27PTS
1973	QUAL FINAL	MCG	RICH V CAR	ATT	86,386	LOSS	20PTS
	1st SEMI FINAL	MCG	RICH V STK	ATT	86,483	WIN	20PTS
	PRE FINAL	MCG	RICH V COLL	ATT	98,652	WIN	7PTS
	GRAND FINAL	MCG	RICH V CAR	ATT	119,956	WIN	80PTS
1974	2nd SEMI FINAL	WAV	RICH V NTH M	ATT	57,569	WIN	21PTS
	GRAND FINAL	MCG	RICH V NTH M	ATT	113,839	WIN	41PTS
1975	E. FINAL	WAV	RICH V COLL	ATT	65,512	WIN	4PTS
	1st SEMI FINAL	MCG	RICH V CAR	ATT	76,967	WIN	9PTS
	PRE FINAL	WAV	RICH V NTH M	ATT	71,130	LOSS	17PTS
1976	**TOM HAFEY**	**10 WINS - 12 LOSSES 98.6%**	*GOODBYE TOMMY*				
	KEVIN SHEEDY	**10 WINS - 12 LOSSES 92.23%**	*GOODBYE KEVIN*				
1977	2nd SEMI FINAL	MCG	COLL V HAW	ATT	87,421	WIN	2PTS
	GRAND FINAL	MCG	COLL V NTH M	ATT	108,224	DRAW	
	GRANDFINAL	MCG	COLL NTH M	ATT	98,491	LOSS	27PTS
1978	QUAL FINAL	MCG	COLL HAW	ATT	97,931	LOSS	56PTS
	1st SEMI FINAL	MCG	COLL V CAR	ATT	91,933	WIN	15PTS
	PRE FINAL	WAV	COLL V NTH M	ATT	73,354	LOSS	12PTS
1979	QUAL FINAL	MCG	COLL V NTH M	ATT	84,660	LOSS	39PTS
	1st SEMI FINAL	MCG	COLL V FITZ	ATT	87,139	WIN	22PTS
	PRE FINAL	WAV	COLL NTH M	ATT	73,380	WIN	27PTS
	GRAND FINAL	MCG	COLL V CAR	ATT	113,545	LOSS	5PTS
1980	ELIM FINAL	MCG	COLL NTH M	ATT	83,033	WIN	8PTS
	1st SEMI FINAL	MCG	COLL V CARL	ATT	94,451	WIN	50PTS
	PRE FINAL	WAV	COLL V GEE	ATT	75,526	WIN	81PTS
	GRANDFINAL	MCG	COLL V RICH	ATT	113,461	LOSS	81PTS
1981	QUAL FINAL	MCG	COLL V GEE	ATT	83,899	LOSS	14PTS
	1st SEMI FINAL	MCG	COLL V FITZ	ATT	85,133	WIN	1PT
	PRE FINAL	WAV	COLL V GEE	ATT	69,536	WIN	7PTS
	GRAND FINAL	MCG	COLL V CAR	ATT	112,964	LOSS	20PTS
1982	AFTER 6 YEARS LEAVES COLLINGWOOD						
	COLL 4WINS - 85% POOR SEASON - 5 GRANDIAL FINAL APPEARANCE						
1983	GEELONG	9TH	8 WINS - 14 LOSSES	87.90%			
1984	GEELONG	6TH	11 WIN - 11 LOSSES	94.30%			
1985	GEELONG	6TH	12 WINS - 10 LOSSES	100.60%			
	LEAVES GEELONG A WINNING SEASON						
1986	SYDNEY	4TH (FINISHES 2nd ON LADDER) H/WAY					
	QUAL FINAL	MCG	SYD V CAR	ATT	66,016	LOSS	16PTS
	1st SEMI	MCG	SYD V FITZ	ATT	65,763	LOSS	5PTS
1987	SYDNEY	4TH (FINISHES 3rd ON LADDER) H/WAY					
	QUAL FINAL	WAV	SYD V HAW	ATT	47,752	LOSS	99PTS
	1stSEMI	MCG	SYD V MELB	ATT	80,292	LOSS	76PTS
1988	SYDNEY	7TH	12 WIN - 10 LOSSES	99.70%			
	LEAVES SYDNEY A WINNING SEASON						

AVERAGE CROWD ATTENDANCE | 89,507

OPPOSITE: *With Tom Hafey's wife, Maureen. Tom coached the team but Maureen fed us, looked after us, and made sure Tom looked after us too. She was the inspiration behind Tom's success and was loved by every player at every club Tommy coached.*

LEFT: *You only have to look at the record of attendances at Tom Hafey's finals games to see his success. It was incredible how often he filled the MCG. In July of 1987 he coached Sydney through three magnificent games where the team scored a total of 97 goals 54 – incredible. But Tom himself would have thought his greatest contribution was promoting health and fitness among ordinary Australians. He would have done more talks around Australia than any other person.*

LEFT: Tom Hafey stressed that it was always important to chat with umpires, get to know them. Here I am taking notes. I've always loved taking notes – it doesn't mean I'm not listening.

TOP RIGHT: The man, the coach. Tommy Hafey was loved by all his players, and his crowds were unbelievable. A superstar for the people.

BOTTOM RIGHT: Tommy Hafey always spoke with his eyes, and he'd look right into you to see if you got the message. Not many people could do that.

3

BACK-POCKET PLUMBER

That's what Tom Hafey used to call me. Harsh call, Coach, after I kicked eight goals, seven in grand finals for you. I love telling Matthew Lloyd that we both kicked nine goals in grand finals, and he just looks at me strange.

FROM FAILURE TO TRIUMPH

BY 1971, AMID GREAT CONTROVERSY, BILLY Barrot had been traded to St Kilda and Ian Stewart brought to Punt Road from Moorabbin, where he had already won two Brownlow Medals. Essentially, Richmond had pulled a swiftie on the Saints. Stewart had told them he wanted to go to Perth, so they thought they needed someone to replace him. The Tiger hierarchy had decided that Barrot, who would probably be diagnosed with depression these days, was hard work, and through Alan Schwab they were quietly letting St Kilda know they might be agreeable to letting Billy go. As soon as that became public, Stewart asked for a transfer to Richmond, to which St Kilda reluctantly agreed. Regardless of what the Richmond management thought of Barrot, he was popular with the supporters and there were public meetings asking to have him brought back. But when Ian won his third Brownlow in 1971 all that was forgotten.

We lost the 1972 Grand Final and, like everyone else at Richmond, Tommy said it took him months to get over it. I was devastated. I had taken to going to the MCG the day before a grand final, sitting in the empty stands and imagining how the game would play out. I hadn't imagined us losing a high-scoring game – 28 goals to 22 – but the Carlton coach John Nicholls had. We were the favourites, we had beaten Carlton in the semi-finals. Nicholls thought the only way to beat us was for Carlton to score as many goals as possible. He got six of his own.

We threw ourselves into preparing for the 1973 season. When we made the grand final, Ian Stewart and I vowed to get at least five of those goals that might have won the 1972 premiership. Along with Royce Hart we got three each. Mine all came in the first quarter, and in the end it was Carlton's turn to be devastated: 16.20 (116) to 12.14 (86). Francis Bourke, one of the great people at Richmond, who is often forgotten because there were so many champions at that time, described it as sweet revenge.

Francis's story was a bit like mine. He was off a dairy farm in Nathalia but he didn't like milking cows all that much, so just as football was my way of getting out of digging ditches and standing in brown stuff, it was his way of getting out of milking cows and standing in brown stuff – if he was good enough. Five premierships say he was and explains why he was known at St Francis after St Francis of Assisi, the patron saint of animals, even though Francis Bourke didn't love animals, particularly cows. There is a St Kevin, an Irish saint, but no one ever thought to call me a saint in my playing days. I still wonder why. 🏉

Geoff Southby is dragged to his feet after being downed by Neil Balme in the 1973 Grand Final against Carlton – I was just checking to see if it was a hard hit. It was unnecessary, Mr Balme.

Paul Feltham pushes the ball into my face in the 1974 Grand Final against North Melbourne. Would you have guessed he ended up becoming a psychologist? Fancy trying to upset me like that. Luckily I rarely got wound up; I always just kept playing sensible football. Nothing could upset me, except for disloyal people.

1974 FLAG AND THE BATTLE OF WINDY HILL

BY 1974, THE TIME OF MY THIRD VFL PREMIERSHIP AS A player, Ian Stewart had retired as the only player to win Brownlow Medals and premierships at two clubs. His retirement came halfway through the season, despite petitions from supporters asking him to change his mind. I wonder how many of those petitioners were the same people who attended the public meetings to bring back Billy Barrot?

One of Ian's last games was at Windy Hill, where he kicked five goals in between one of the biggest brawls you have ever seen at a footy game. Some might be surprised, but I had no part in that brawl – though I was an interested spectator. Kevin Bartlett says he couldn't even look, but it's more likely that 'Hungry' was more focused on getting off the ground to the afternoon tea before anyone else.

There were police horses on the ground; there were general managers on the ground. Graeme Richmond was charged with assault causing actual bodily harm and unlawful assault, but both charges were eventually dropped, which meant the ban on him working with the club for the rest of the season also had to be lifted. Graeme had his connections, we always knew that.

It was a case of having connected rather than connections for Ronnie Andrews, and he was suspended for six weeks by the VFL tribunal. The Essendon player who broke the jaw of Brian 'The Whale' Roberts got off because Brian wouldn't dob him in.

The Bombers' runner Laurie Ashley and fitness coach Jim Bradley were also penalised: Bradley for whacking Mal Brown, who also got a week for belting Ashley, while my teammate Stephen Parsons got a week for hitting Bradley. Nothing like that would ever happen now (though Essendon might have got close in the 1990 Grand Final).

The grand final in 1974 was always going to be a tough one. North Melbourne had gone on one of the biggest recruiting sprees in the history of the game. Ron Barassi was the coach and under the 10-year-rule, a 1970s version of free agency, the Kangaroos had been able to recruit Doug Wade from Geelong, Barry Davis from Essendon and John 'Mopsy' Rantall from South Melbourne. They already had a brilliant player from Western Australia, Barry Cable, and Keith Greig won the Brownlow Medal that year.

We had finished top of the ladder and had beaten North in the second semi-final

This brawl had everything. Probably the best cage fight I've ever seen, without the cage. Some of the greatest names in football were there. What a great shot; you can see the faces in the crowd. The little kid on the ground makes me think, 'Geez how unorganised were we back then?' Thank God it wouldn't happen today. Wouldn't you like to interview that young man today? What were his thoughts being so close to the action? If you're out there, I'd love to meet you.

so we were feeling confident, but they were leading by 12 points in the second quarter when I took a one-handed mark in the forward pocket. The angle was so acute and the gap between the posts so narrow that it looked like the ball would get stuck rather than go through, but I went back to take my kick anyway. Then, while running in, I saw that Michael Green was unmarked in the goal square, so I handballed over the man on the mark, and Michael kicked an easy goal. The commentators said Richmond lifted from then and North didn't recover, and we went on to win by 41 points. It was just as well Kevin Bartlett hadn't taken that mark, because there's no way he would have handballed it (only joking, KB). 🏉

OPPOSITE: *Against Wayne Judson, St Kilda, 1974. An unusual photo because there are two back pockets playing on each other. At least I was going the right way.*

TOP: *Leigh Matthews, 1973, when the Hawks could never get to Richmond – which used to annoy Don Scott. I always loved playing on Leigh, he always brought out the best in you. Going up against a player like Leigh is a really great opportunity to test yourself, because you have to lift to beat a champion.*

BOTTOM: *I always took the pre-season comp seriously, more seriously than most, as a player and a coach. If you're going to be in it, you're going to be in it to win it. Graeme Richmond taught me that.*

ABOVE: 1974. My best ever mark in a grand final. With one hand I outmarked my teammate Michael Green, who made the Richmond team of the century. I went back for the shot – and probably would have got it despite the really tight angle – but handballed to Michael instead for a certain goal. That turned the momentum in the match and we never looked back. Michael and Francis Bourke are two of the best people in AFL history. We used to practise one-handed marks at training, just in case a player was holding onto you. In cricket you'd call it a slips cordon catch between second slip and gully – in AFL you just call it a mark.

LEFT: And my second-best mark in a grand final (I only took two), also in 1974. The picture was taken from the wall of the Richmond museum.

ABOVE: On the receiving end of a lecture from university professor Ian Robinson in the 1974 Grand Final. Taking orders from a scholar wasn't easy for a plumber. Far left is Paul Sproule, one of my favourite Tigers players.

OPPOSITE TOP: Great shots, great era. Alan Schwab was general manager of Richmond, and he was a fantastic visionary and inspiration to me. He really created opportunities for Richmond in the late '60s and early '70s, and was a terrific complement to Hafey. The trading and swapping of players was his greatest strength, and he was one of the best at developing the game.

OPPOSITE BOTTOM: That was a tremendously successful era where Richmond got three flags in a row, culminating in this 1974 side. It was a hard team to beat. To be in three grand finals in row and to take it from Ron Barassi's North Melbourne was a great effort.

A TASTE OF LEADERSHIP

BEING CAPTAIN OF RICHMOND IN 1978 FOR ONE year was a great learning experience that prepared me for coaching. I would have loved to have done a better job leading the Tigers, but foolishly I expected everyone to be dedicated, not to drink too much and to do what the coach says. We had a lot of different characters at Richmond. Some you didn't have to worry about too much, others you had to keep an eye on. I didn't realise that until too late.

It's a funny thing at Richmond that most of the captains didn't last that long – but then, after Tommy Hafey, most of the coaches didn't either. Roger Dean was captain when we won the flag in 1969, Royce Hart had the job from 1972 to 1975, but then Bryan Wood, Kevin Bartlett, Francis Bourke and I all had a turn. Maybe it was Richmond's way of giving us leadership experience. After all, Royce, Kevin, Francis and I all became coaches.

The captains at Richmond were all good people, and as coach that's what I was always looking for in my captains. I wanted people who were natural leaders in terms of their attitude and professionalism, who understood that a team is made up of a lot of different characters. The list of captains at Essendon in my time is a pretty good one: Simon Madden, Neale Daniher, Terry Daniher, Tim Watson, Mark Thompson, Gary O'Donnell, Michael Long, James Hird. It's a pretty good list at Greater Western Sydney too: Luke Power, Callan Ward and Phil Davis.

BACK ROW: Royce Har
Ala
MIDDLE ROW: Gary Davidson, Ian Scrim
SEATED: Francis Bourke,
Barry Richardson (Coach),
FRONT ROW: Jon H

RICHMOND FOOTBALL CLUB 1978

...alist Coach), Wayne Walsh, Jim Jess, Bruce Monteath, Michael Roach, David Cloke,
...rds, Eric Leech, Peter Laughlin, Tony Jewell (Assistant Coach).
...Mervyn Keane, Cameron Clayton, Mark Lee, Robert Heard, Robert McGhie, Neil Balme, Barry Grinter.
...Bartlett (Vice-Captain), Paul Feltham, Kevin Sheedy (Captain), Ian Wilson (President),
...Andrews (General Manager), Glen Dickson, Bryan Wood, Brian LeBrocq (Team Manager).
...Stephen Rae, Michael Malthouse, Geoff Raines, Robert Lamb, Ken Stonehouse.

This was my first year as captain at Richmond. With the talent we had there, I was very, very fortunate.

It was probably because of my dedication that they made me captain in 1978. It was the only time I ever beat Bartlett at anything. He thought they'd read out the wrong Kevin and soon pointed out that he was a better player and that he should have been captain. He was right.

Other highlights of my time at Richmond include the 1978 tour of Ireland with Harry Beitzel's Galahs. I didn't go on the first ones in 1967 and 1968 because Harry was an umpire at that stage and didn't like me much, but he warmed to me over the years. Breaking my ankle on that tour didn't exactly endear me to the Richmond hierarchy, and there was a general sense around this time that some of them were going for me and that my feet were firmly planted over Graeme Richmond's infamous Punt Road trapdoor. So I needed to make plans for a future after playing.

Talking in riddles

I thought Kevin was a bit rough around the edges when I met him through my husband, Graeme, when he began playing for Richmond back in the 1960s. He had no teeth and was tough-looking, but I think that was what Graeme liked most about Kevin – the toughness. Kevin had a very competitive nature, not just in games but also in training, and Graeme liked that about him too. He thought if you were like that at training, crashing into your teammates, you would be hard on the opposition on match day.

Graeme was famous for his recruiting, particularly the polite way he went about it. He was always well-mannered and got on very well with the parents of the players. Many of the new players even lived with him until they found their own accommodation. He had brought some very good players to Richmond, like Royce Hart from Tasmania. There's a famous story about how Graeme got the deal over the line by promising Mr and Mrs Hart that he would buy Royce some new clothes.

Graeme also knew that sometimes he alone could not entice parents to let their sons go to Richmond, so he would take club legends like Jack Dyer or Roy Wright along, believing that parents would be so impressed at having them in their living rooms, they would find it hard to say no. Kevin went on a lot of recruiting excursions with Graeme as he became better known, and he learned Graeme's assessment system: 1. Good chance, 2. Won't make it, 3. Possible, 4. Unlikely, 5. Could not handle the training.

Graeme also enlisted Kevin's mother, Irene, into his recruiting programs. She would board some of the new players and quietly assess them according to Graeme's system, then she'd pass along her thoughts.

I saw Kevin mature over his time at Richmond, but by the time he was heading off for his interview for the coaching job at Essendon, he still had a few of those rough edges I saw when I first met him. He was still getting around in a daggy old tracksuit with the knees out of it, so I said, 'Kevin, you've got to get rid of that tracksuit.' He told me later I was right; if he wanted to impress the people at Essendon with his leadership qualities, he had to dress like a leader as well as talk like one.

Even though it was Graeme who called the end of his playing career, I know Kevin always admired him and was grateful for all the opportunities he provided, not just on the field, but in player development and his development as an assistant coach. Graeme knew that Kevin was headed for great things – he is such a different person, even if sometimes he talks in riddles. It is a mark of the great respect that Kevin had for Graeme that he has kept in touch with me and my family, greeting us warmly whenever we meet. Graeme would be very proud of him.

Jan Richmond, wife of Graeme Richmond who was with Richmond in various roles, including vice-president, from 1962 to 1983. Graeme died in 1991.

SPIN DOCTOR

MARK THOMPSON, WHO WAS A PRETTY GOOD left-arm bowler himself, reckons that once in the 1980s, when the Bombers played a social game at Windy Hill against the Essendon Cricket Club, I took the game so seriously that I spent five minutes setting my field. Bomber is right, because I always took my cricket seriously. That had to be the case when, nearing 30, I decided to see how far I could go in the VCA competition – as a leg-spinner. Richie Benaud had been a hero of mine when I was a schoolboy. I had read that when it was done well, leg-spin was the most dangerous of all forms of bowling. The ball would turn away from the right-handed batsman and towards the slips, the cleverly disguised wrong 'un cannoning into the batsman's pads – or, even better, his stumps. Though I would not call my wrong 'un cunningly disguised – rather, it was accidental. If I had no idea which way it was going to turn, then neither did the batsman.

I started in the fourths at Richmond in the 1976–77 season, and by the end of the summer I was in the seconds. People told me I was mad to go to that club, because Jimmy Higgs was their number one leg-spinner. But Sister Rupert's arithmetic helped me again. One into 11 would go if I could work my way up the grades, because when Higgsie was called up to play for Victoria, I might get a game in the firsts. Jim did better than that: he got chosen for Australia's tour of the West Indies in 1978. By February of that year, with the guidance of another wily spinner – the former Test cricketer George Tribe, who was a coach at Richmond – I had turned myself into a bowler good enough to be regarded as a hopeful replacement for Jim Higgs.

When Jim bowled the ball, it fizzed out of his fingers, while I gave it more of a gentle tweak. But that had been good enough for me to get 13 wickets in five first-grade games at an average of just over 16. So when the

---

Richmond's star footballer Kevin Sheedy has turned his talents to another sport — cricket.

Sheedy was last night selected in Richmond's firsts for the Tigers' District cricket clash against Prahran at Toorak Park tomorrow.

It is the first time Sheedy, a right-arm leg spinner, has been selected in the senior team.

And the match has special interest for Sheedy, 29. He was born and bred in Prahran.

"I could be going home for a killing, but I hope not," he said last night.

Sheedy started his cricket career with net training in the 1975/76 season. During the 1976/77 season, he played with the fourths, thirds and seconds.

"It's been a fairly quick trip to the top in District cricket for me in just two seasons, but the club have been right behind me all the way," he said.

"The players and coach have been great. They're the people I need to thank for this chance in the firsts."

— JOHN LETHLEAN

It was great to be able to break into a district side at 30. I really enjoyed the low-key approach to district cricket compared to being captain at Richmond. Jim Higgs was often away with Australia, and I got to play in lots of great, competitive matches. The infrastructure tactics of cricket were very in tune with VFL – placing a field to get a different bowler out, that sort of thing. It really helped my coaching career later on. The happiest wicket I ever got was Keith Stackpole, and other highlights were getting Graeme Wood out caught behind (by Boon) at Geoff Marsh's testimonial match in front of 20,000 at the WACA.

That was a great district cricket team at Richmond, full of distinguished cricketers. You won't thank me naming them all, but among that crowd are the likes of David Cowper, who has played the most games of district cricket and first-class matches for Victoria; Graham Yallop, who became Australia's 35th Test captain; spinner Jim Higgs who played 22 Tests for Australia; George Tribe who played Test cricket for Australia and 66 games for Footscray in the VFL; great captain Jock Irvine; and club icon Peter Williams.

final came along and Richmond was set to play Carlton, I was pretty certain I would get a game and possibly become the first person to win a premiership in the VFL and the VCA. At that time there were plenty of people who could have done it, but no one had. They included South Melbourne's Brownlow Medallist Peter Bedford, who also played 39 games for Victoria as a leg-spinning all-rounder. It was a lot easier to combine cricket and football at a high level back then. The Australian opening bowlers on the Invincibles' tour of England, Ray Lindwall and Keith Miller, did it. Lindwall, a goal-kicking fullback (a contradiction in terms in Australian Rules Football) played in a losing grand final for St George in the 1942 Sydney Rugby League competition, while Miller played 50 games in the VFL for St Kilda.

Back to the VCA final, if I was to play in this match, which was close to the start of the footy season, I would need to get approval from the Tigers. Unfortunately, people in power at Punt Road – it might have been Graeme Richmond, it might have been Ian Wilson, or it might have been Barry Richardson, I have never been sure – said no. It's one of the biggest regrets of my life, and one of the reasons I always let the Bombers play cricket if they wanted to. The Richmond Cricket Club went into that grand final without a spinner of any type, and they lost. To this day I still wonder whether the result might have been different if they had a bowler who could turn the ball away towards the slips, before slipping in an accidental wrong' un.

A competitive beast

Kevin Sheedy did for the AFL what we were trying to achieve back in 1977 when the best of Australia's cricketers signed up for Kerry Packer's World Series Cricket. We wanted to play the most competitive form of cricket we could, and in the most entertaining way.

Nobody would deny Kevin Sheedy's competitiveness – you don't win three premierships as a player and four as a coach without being a competitive beast – but he was also responsible for making the game more entertaining, particularly through wonderful initiatives like the Anzac Day match and Dreamtime at the 'G. I doubt the AFL would be where it is today – as the number one winter sport – without the Sheedy mix of playing hard but making it a lot of fun as well.

Kevin is a keen cricket fan, and we met for the first time in the Australian cricket team's dressing room. On another occasion we were on his patch when Tom Hafey invited Rodney Marsh and myself down to Punt Road to give the Richmond players a motivational talk. We ended up doing a promotional photo shoot with Kevin out on the ground, having a kick and not doing too badly from memory, as Rod and I had both been pretty good junior footballers.

Over the years I have continued to bump into Kevin at airports and places like that, and we always have a good conversation. I have developed the greatest respect for what he has done in his career.

He was probably a better coach than a player, and he was probably the best motivational coach the game has ever seen or heard. In some ways he is probably a better salesman than he is a coach.

I barrack for the West Coast Eagles and I know the difficulties they had in their early days in the AFL, when they started out training at Floreat Park in Perth and had none of the facilities that players take for granted these days, like hydro baths, lap pools and medical facilities.

It was much the same thing when Kevin became the foundation coach of Greater Western Sydney, because the Giants had no permanent facilities and were often training in parks around Sydney's west. There were a few senior players, but the squad then was mostly made up of teenagers who needed to be taught the game. Despite those humble beginnings, I knew it would work with Kevin in charge.

You can see from where they are now how well he did, but of course being Kevin, he did more than that; being the super-salesman as well as coach, he went out and got sponsorships for the Giants and took an interest in the building of the new stadium that would be their permanent home. I can't think of any other coach who could have done what Kevin has done in Greater Western Sydney, just by the sheer force of his personality.

Dennis Lillee AM MBE, former Australian Test cricketer.

FAREWELL RICHMOND

MILESTONES ARE VERY IMPORTANT IN football. As a coach, it was always my aim to get a player to 100 games, as in the case of Dean Rioli, or 200 games, as with Mark Thompson. These milestones are measurements of a footballer's courage, perseverance and ability.

My 251 games for Richmond say that I was a very determined person who was lucky enough to play alongside some of the best footballers of our generation. But this milestone came with some bitterness.

Richmond was no longer the same club that I had joined – for a start, Tom Hafey wasn't there anymore. On top of that, the club had refused to let me play in the cricket grand final. After that decision, in one of the best moves in my career, I demanded that the club either sign a release or I would never play for Richmond again. President Ian Wilson agreed, but he must have forgotten about it, because when I was offered a role at Essendon as the VFL's first full-time coach, he said there was no way he would let me go. But it was too late: the release had been signed, and I was ready for something new. Richmond had been fantastic to me; Tom Hafey, Graeme Richmond and Alan Schwab had given me opportunities for which I am forever grateful, but coaching, and Essendon, were calling. 🏉

ABOVE: Waverley in 1979. The Tigers fans were fantastic to players on their milestone games. It's a wonderfully important moment for players, and they really appreciate the effort fans put into the banners. (The Giants fans are unbelievable; they come from miles away to do their banners, and the team have only been there for five years.)

OPPOSITE: Final game for Richmond at Waverley Park in 1979. You always think you've got more to offer. Carlton wanted me to play for them, and I had open clearance to go, but I was determined to proudly be a one-club player. The mighty Blues won it that year, but Richmond won it the following year, and it was great to be part of that as an assistant coach. Eighteen months later, I was coach at Essendon.

I probably should have been fined for not wearing Nubrik on my jumper. This group of players took Essendon to two premierships.

4

BECOMING A BOMBER

Tony Jewell and the team let me become assistant coach in my final year at Richmond. I got to see at close quarters Richmond's amazing turnaround from fifth bottom to the biggest win in grand final history. I stole nothing when I went to Essendon, but I borrowed quite a bit!

The view from the outer

We interviewed Kevin twice for the position of Essendon coach, both times at the home of the then-president, Colin Stubbs. Kevin had obviously done his homework and knew the club inside and out, particularly the roles of the interviewing panel members – Colin Stubbs, chairman of selectors Brian Donohoe, General Manager Roy McConnell and me – and he wasn't frightened to let us know. We thought he was a bit cocky, but talking to him later, he felt he was merely showing us how much confidence he had in having properly prepared himself for the job he had been working towards for years – a full-time coaching role in football.

He thinks the strangest question of all was the one from Roy McConnell: 'Do you mind if people smoke in the change rooms after the game?' Smoking and drinking were very much part of the game back then – in fact Kevin, Brian and I would laugh together when Bob Syme, the coach of reserves, would take out hip flasks at half-time ... purely medicinal of course, as it got cold at Windy Hill in those days and you didn't want your players catching a chill.

At the end of those two job interviews, the panel got together and decided to go for Kevin ahead of Allan Jeans. We thought Kevin was more a man of the 1980s, but of course Allan also won plenty of premierships in that decade at Hawthorn. Still, Kevin got us two premierships in 1984 and 1985, and what wonderful times they were for the club.

Neville Gay, long-time Essendon committeeman and a member of the panel that employed Kevin at Essendon.

Graeme Johnston, myself, Brian Donohoe, Bernie Sheehy (a fantastic assistant coach who I made assistant coach of Victoria – Ted Whitten didn't like that because Bernie had never played) watching a game against North Melbourne in 1982. Observing the enemy is the start of every strategy for success.

WINNING THEM OVER

THE COMMITTEE OF COLIN STUBBS, BRIAN DONOHOE, Neville Gay and Roy McConnell recommended me for the job over Allan Jeans. Fourteen board members voted to approve my appointment, with one abstention – a person known around the club as St Thomas, the doubting apostle. There would be battles, no question about that.

Not everyone at Essendon liked the idea of a full-time coach for starters, and not everyone at Essendon liked the idea that this new full-time coach was Kevin Sheedy.

Even though I didn't throw a punch in 1974's 'Battle of Windy Hill', I had been on the other side, and that was enough for many Bomber people. Over the years, a lot of them would come up to me and say, 'I used to hate you when you were at Richmond, I thought you were such a dirty player. But now you're at Essendon and I've got to know you, you're not that bad.'

> I had no idea how long it would take to win people over, but I was pretty sure it would happen faster if the Bombers started winning games of football.

They hadn't won a premiership since 1965 and I felt like the club was in a sort of a stall – happy to be ordinary, happy to make the finals and be eliminated in the first weeks, even happy to just miss the finals. That wasn't me.

The players weren't skilled enough, they weren't fit enough and they weren't ruthless enough. So I decided they had to become more like the Richmond I'd known: skilled, fit, ruthless and with a hatred of losing.

'Brian, how many games do I need to give you to make sure that if your young fella can play we can recruit him under the father–son rule?' Talking it through with Brian Brown, father of Jonathan.

I always say, never knock back a kid who's asking for an autograph – they're the future of the game. Early on at my time with the Giants, I took photos of the players' scrawls and made it clear that if you act disinterested and give a kid a lazy spaghetti autograph they won't remember you well. It was one of the most important training sessions we had: do not disrespect any kid's ambitions.

Persistence pays off

When I came to Essendon as chairman of selectors, I saw it as a way to give back to the club that I had barracked for since I was a youngster, wagging school at Assumption College in Kilmore to go and watch Dick Reynolds break Jack Dyer's record for most games in the VFL. The Marist Brothers weren't impressed and I got six cuts with the cane, but it was worth it. Sport, cricket as well as football, were far more important to me than schoolwork, which probably explains why I spent most of my life in football, even at a club where Catholics could be made to feel unwelcome. I know when Kevin told Graeme Richmond he was going to Essendon, Graeme told him he wouldn't last five minutes 'with the Masons over there'.

I was on the panel that interviewed Kevin, and it says a lot about how well he did in the interviews because, despite being a Catholic, he got the job. Kevin knew exactly what he needed to develop his players into premiership champions. One of the questions we asked him in the interview was who he thought were our most skilful players. We were a bit shocked, considering we had players on our list like Tim Watson, when he told us we didn't have any skilful players. He then added, 'What you do have is plenty of potentially skilful players.'

When he started as coach, one of the first things Kevin did was demand that every player be given his own ball to help develop his skills. That horrified the club treasurer, as footballs were expensive. But Kevin, with a fair bit of support from me behind the scenes, got his way. Soon it was being said around Windy Hill that the Masons were raising the money and the Catholics were spending it. Kevin always acknowledges that in those early days I took a lot of knives for him. He was still inexperienced in the workings of a football club, particularly the politics. Whenever he was asked to present to the board, I'd make sure I had a few Dorothy Dixers ready for him, and then get him out of the room as fast as I could.

Then, to liven things up even further for me, there were the arguments I had with Kevin. After the win in the first game of the night series in 1981, he told me he was going to play in the next one. He thought he could be out there with the players and tell them what to do. We had a discussion over that one, and in the end he didn't play, something that he did eventually concede was the right decision. He had been out of the game for too long.

Another time, after I stormed out of a selection meeting, I rang him the next day and said, 'You're the coach, it's your decision, but make sure you get it right.' The player was Paul Weston, who Kevin wanted to play in the centre while the other option was fullback. In the end, he played in the centre in the first half and fullback after half-time. Maybe Kevin won the argument slightly. The coach should always be tested.

One Saturday in the early 1980s we were training for a Monday game against Carlton. Ronnie Andrews was missing – gone pig shooting. What should we do? We could drop him, but the smell of a victory over Carlton was hard to resist. Come Monday, Ronnie played after a tongue-lashing in front of the team, and we won. I suspect, though, that lack of dedication was the reason Andrews wasn't picked to play in the 1983 Grand Final.

In his early days at the club, Kevin was headstrong, and some might argue he has never changed. At one stage he had decided to wear the black tracksuit and footy boots on match days. I think he worked out for himself how different he looked. Years later, I showed him and the players a video of Kevin in this gear. The players got a laugh out of it, and I think Kevin might have too.

Everyone knows what a great ambassador Kevin has been for football. He has ideas about how to promote the game, but he also has the drive to get them implemented. A lot of people weren't convinced about the Anzac Day game, but Kevin kept persevering until he found others who were interested – Collingwood, as it turned out. It's the same with the Dreamtime at the 'G, and now the Country Game. It took seven years to get that up and running. If nothing else, Kevin is persistent.

Another reason he has been such a successful promoter of our sport is that he never criticises the game. He might criticise some of the decisions of the AFL, or other clubs, but he always talks up Australian football. Once I used to say, 'Where would Essendon be if it wasn't for Kevin Sheedy?' These days I say, 'Where would Australian football be if it wasn't for Kevin?'

Brian Donohoe, a former Essendon player who was chairman of selectors when Kevin first joined the club.

Neville Gay (left) and Brian Donohoe(middle) – old friends who were a huge part of me getting started at Essendon.

TAKING FROM THE TIGERS

TOMMY HAFEY USED TO SAY THAT ON LEAVING Richmond to coach at Essendon, I took everything that wasn't nailed down. And why not? Along with Carlton, Richmond was the most successful club in the game at that time – five premierships between 1967 and 1980 say the Tigers must have been doing something right!

There was heaps to pilfer from Tommy Hafey about fitness, but also about trying out players in different positions. (I didn't mind a bit that people were calling me Kevin Hafey.) At Richmond we knew that wonderful feeling of running away with a game in the final quarter because we were fitter than our opponents. We also enjoyed the fact that we won grand finals because Tommy would play people like Barry Richardson, Dick Clay and Francis Bourke in different positions in different grand finals just to keep the opposition guessing.

From Graeme Richmond came the idea that you had to be fearless and ruthless. The rumour that he had a trapdoor in his office came about because when he felt a player was not giving his all or was past his best, he would call them into his office and the player would never be seen again.

From Alan Schwab, along with Graeme Richmond, came the knowledge that you must be a good recruiter. Alan played a crucial and clever role in getting Ian Stewart to Richmond.

Unsung hero Bill Boromeo was our sprint coach at Richmond and a big part of our success. Every summer, we'd do athletics training, and most of the team would end up running somewhere around Victoria in the pro athletics. Bartlett was the best. It meant that at Essendon I knew our dedication during off-season was going to change our performance. Now it's taken for granted, but it was a new idea then. Peter Power, our fitness coach at Essendon, really enhanced the Bombers' fitness training. The players hated it (until they won a premiership).

Noel Judkins, the man who first identified Michael Long as a future champion and one of the best people in football, came over too. Noel was to be the first full-time recruiting manager at Essendon, and he stayed with the club for three premierships and five grand finals.

Eventually, along came my premiership teammate Kevin Morris, who coached the reserves to a grand final win in 1983, along with Dr Rudi Webster, the former first-class cricketer who had been the manager for the West Indian cricket team and psychologist for the Tigers. Another idea loaned from Richmond was that every player should have his own ball so that he could develop his skills.

The final thing that made it from Punt Road to Windy Hill was the determination that had made me a premiership player against all the odds. I guess it was partly that determination that saw me appointed as the first full-time coach the game ever had, even though I had barely any coaching experience at all. And I was determined to do everything required to succeed as coach.

Recruiting staff was another thing I took from Richmond, and hooking up around Australia with a new recruitng team under Noel Judkins was critically important. Noel went everywhere and had a great eye for players.

Some motivation for my 1983 team: if you keep working hard, one day you too could be showering with the cup.

Thinking outside the square

I became an Essendon supporter because, growing up in Adelaide, I followed West Adelaide, whose colours are red and black. I followed all the red and black teams in Australia, including North Sydney in the Sydney Rugby League competitions and Wests Rugby League team in Brisbane.

When I first met Kevin Sheedy it was at a Cricket Australia function. I wasn't surprised to see him there. I knew of his interest in leg-spin bowling as Jimmy Higgs's understudy at Richmond Cricket Club. I can recall having a lengthy discussion in which I spent most of the time listening to him tell me what a great leg-spinner he was.

Thereafter we would catch up infrequently, sometimes because of my interest in Essendon, other times because of his interest in cricket. One of those meetings comes readily to mind. In 2000 I was back living in Adelaide and coaching the South Australian team. I came to Melbourne for a golfing trip, and was happy to see that Essendon was playing North Melbourne at the MCG on Sunday.

I had arranged with Peter Jackson, CEO of Essendon, to get tickets to the 'G, and went out to Windy Hill (with Jack Clarke, who went on to be chairman of Cricket Australia) to pick them up. As we left Peter's office, I noticed that the players were training, so we stood and watched them for a while. As the players were leaving the field, Robert Shaw recognised me and invited us into the rooms.

Robert knew full well that Kevin was always pleased to see anyone for a chat, particularly if he could bring up his leg-spin

again, so we went up to Kevin's little office and heard about Kevin's cricket prowess. I was more interested in getting reassurance about Essendon's season. We were heading into round 13 and the Bombers were doing well, but there was always that nagging thing with Kevin that he would get carried away and start playing the backline in the forward line and the forward line in the backline and mess up a good season.

Kevin told us what he was planning, and it all sounded good. By way of reassurance, possibly, he invited us into a team meeting: 'The players have got a meeting about Sunday's game, and the coaches don't have any involvement; it will be run by James.' James was James Hird, the club captain, and the meeting was around a mini ground that had been marked out in white tape on the floor. James and the players were talking about their game plan coming out of defence, and how if the ball was on the ground to be won and two or three players from each side were around it, the nearest player should go for the ball and the other two go left and right ready to take the handball.

On the Sunday, we went to the MCG and we were sitting in the Southern Stand back pocket. At quarter time Essendon led seven to nil – it was like a training run, as if North had not turned up. Where we were sitting we could watch that game plan in action, and it was working exactly how James and the other players said it would.

Essendon ended up winning the game by eight goals, so that first quarter was critical, the game becoming more even as it went on. The thing that really intrigued me was that the game plan still worked

There's no doubt I'm outgoing, and I get particularly excited when I meet people I admire, which was probably a strange experience for a quiet person like Greg Chappell. I've always believed that different sports should learn from each other in coaching; take whatever you like and add it to your coaching bin. The most important thing about cricket that AFL players need to learn is concentration – people don't talk about it enough in the art of AFL performance.

when the game was on equal footing; a good plan is only really a good plan when the players can stick to it under pressure.

I thought to myself with a smile, 'Well, the players aren't going to let the coaches stuff it up this year.' They didn't: in 2000 Essendon won the grand final. James had a very strong influence on that, and despite what we might think of Kevin's fascination with making too many moves, there's no doubt he was the main driver of that success, empowering the players, but always making sure they stuck to the game plan.

There were many days, though, when I would be swearing at the television because Kevin did something I thought was detrimental to the way the team was playing. But there were more days when I thought what he had done was exceptional.

That was his great strength and weakness as a coach: his creativity and his ability to think outside the square. I can remember a couple of other occasions when we ran into each other and I walked away amazed at his mind. It works on a different level to others.

As we know through the way he brought Indigenous players into the game, the Anzac Day match and so many other innovations, Kevin has had a huge impact not just on Essendon but on Australian football. Look what he has helped start with Greater Western Sydney.

It's great to see him back at the Essendon Football Club, because after some tough times, even if he is not the coach any more, it still gives one a lot of faith in the future.

Greg Chappell, former Australian Test cricket captain and Bombers supporter.

OPPOSITE TOP and BOTTOM:
Fitzroy Gardens. All of a sudden I got
married and a family started popping
up like rabbits. Suddenly kids were
coming from everywhere. Geraldine was
sensational, because I wasn't home much
and most of the work of the family was
done by her. In a fair assessment, my
dedication to coaching meant I wasn't
the most dedicated parent, but Geraldine
held the fort well.

ABOVE and RIGHT: Fun with Jessica
and Sam, the youngest two. Sam turned
up in September and made it awkward
for a premiership. First two kids arrived
within three years – good effort, Geraldine.
I haven't been home since.

Still promoting the vests in the 1980s – it's important to support the wool industry. A hot day at three-quarter time of a big game, and I just wanted players to concentrate, even though they were tired. Number 25 was the great Roger Merrett. I gave him the number of Ken Timms, one of my top Bomber players. I'd often do this when my players reminded me of old favourites.

5

THE 1980S

Essendon didn't have the right attitude to the game when I arrived, so I had to work hard to get them out of their slump and into the mind-frame of winners. It was high stakes because there were plenty waiting for me to fail.

1983 – BREAK THROUGH OR BREAK DOWN

IN 1983 WE MADE IT TO THE GRAND FINAL, ONLY to be destroyed by the Hawks – 140 to a dismal 57. That loss was a big disappointment in more ways than one. It showed me that a big change in attitude needed to happen if Essendon was going to have a real shot at premiership.

At Richmond, we were gutted after losing the 1972 Grand Final to Carlton, and that inspired us for 1973 and 1974. I didn't get that same feeling from the Essendon players when we lost the 1983 Grand Final to Hawthorn, and by the record margin of 20.20 (140) to 8.9 (57). And I'd lost to Allan Jeans too!

You didn't need 20/20 vision to see that while the Bombers had got better since 1981, we still had a long way to go. We had celebrated winning the preliminary final against North Melbourne like that was good enough. To me it wasn't anywhere near good enough, a feeling I made very clear at the club dinner after that grand final.

'If it doesn't hurt tonight,' I told the room, 'then Essendon will never win another premiership. To put it mildly this was the most disappointing day of my life. I don't want you to enjoy tonight. I hope you all watch the game again. For me, that's what it's all about. That's why I came here. I hope the honest, football-loving people of Essendon realise our hurt and shame because of our shocking and unaccountable grand final performance. That's the way I believe we should feel about today.

'There is no room for excuses when we play games like we did, whether it's during the year or in a grand final – particularly in a grand final! Winning premierships is what football is all about. Winning is the only way to have a really great time. I know it's hard, and you may feel it's hard on your ears, but I don't want you to enjoy yourself tonight. Not at all!'

That was aimed at the players, but there were a lot of people in the room – sponsors, coterie members, various officials – and they were shocked, even angry. In their minds, Essendon people didn't speak to each other that way. I felt like it was a break through or break down moment. While it put my job on the line, it also laid the foundations for what was to happen over the next two years.

OPPOSITE TOP: Coach under fire. Not sure if that was rain – it could have been steam.

OPPOSITE BOTTOM: The Hawks ran away with the 1983 Premiership; we got absolutely slaughtered and it was easily the worst I'd ever felt in my footy life. I was unimpressed to see that the feeling wasn't shared around Essendon that night, but we sorted that out there and then.

This is very much reminiscent of the era, the 80s, with a typical bucket of balls, all different jumpers and tracksuits, and the coach actually talking to the players like this, quite loose. It's a funny shot compared to what you'd see of the organisational set-up these days.

THE 1984 FLAG

SO, THERE WE WERE, 29 SEPTEMBER 1984, back at the MCG.

After we got hammered in the 1983 Premiership and I made myself unpopular with the after-match speech, we'd worked our way to another grand final, the second of three straight that we would play against a Hawthorn coached by Allan Jeans, the man Essendon had turned down for me.

We had been absolutely smashed by Hawthorn the year before, and had made some changes, but not many. We had a couple of young kids on the bench who were largely untried, Mark Thompson and Mark Harvey. Meanwhile, Hawthorn had champions wherever you looked: Leigh Matthews, Gary Ayres, Dermott Brereton, Michael Tuck (an underrated player who I admire enormously). They also had the first four goals of the game. I thought this was another defining moment.

Someone (it might have been me) sent the runner out with a message to start a fight, which some players did better than others. The sight of Simon Madden swinging punches and hitting fresh air is something we still laugh about today. Whether the Hawthorn players were distracted or laughing themselves, the ploy worked and we kicked our first relieving goal. But Hawthorn responded immediately with goals to Brereton and Tuck – 6.1 to 2.4 at quarter time.

This photo from the 1983 grand final (which we lost) is actually where our 1984 Premiership began. It was three-quarter time, and I needed my players to understand that they may never come back to this stadium again in their lifetime. It didn't work that year, but by the next season the message had sunk in.

The boys deserved this. Peter Power, my great fitness coach (in yellow), took the Bombers' fitness levels to an all-time high. He was sensational at really building up the base, and overcoming all the whinging and moaning from the players – I wouldn't be surprised if he's deaf now. He was also our runner back then.

Then the Hawks got the first two goals in the second quarter. As the game wore on, we felt that we were playing as well as them, but just not getting the results on the scoreboard. At half-time we trailed 8.6 to 3.11. The time had come to try something different. Billy Duckworth, who had started at fullback, was pushed forward, Leon Baker went to half-forward and Darren Williams to the middle. Moving players around like this is run-of-the-mill these days but it was quite novel at the time.

It was a goal apiece in the third quarter when in the 18th minute, Billy Duckworth took a great mark over Gary Ayres and David O'Halloran, and grabbed the game by the scruff of the neck. Although Dermie Brereton provided the Hawks with a steadying goal, we went to three-quarter time with a shot of confidence. We were 23 points down, but I felt we were on the up and they were exhausted, and that became my message to the players.

'Have a look at them,' I said, pointing to the Hawthorn huddle. 'They're gone!'

I went around to every one of my players, looked them in the eye and told them the game was in the balance. 'We've got it,' I said, over and over again. 'We've got this, we've got this.' And I could sense that belief growing and growing.

Myself and Tim Watson celebrating after winning the 1984 Grand Final. 'And Sheeds, I'm sorry I said all those things on the training track when you were training the guts out of us.'

At the start of the final quarter Simon Madden, the worst fighter in the history of the game but the best ruckman ever, tapped the ball to Darren Williams, who kicked it towards a scrum of players, from which Leon Baker emerged with the ball and kicked a goal. Then Peter Bradbury took a mark and kicked a goal, and there were just a couple of goals in it. Tim Watson – bless him, I've always loved Timmy – charged down a tired kick from Richard Loveridge, then picked up the ball and fired it to Duckworth who saw Mark Thompson about 40 metres out from where he kicked the goal. A good decision to play the kids. Then another Leon Baker goal and we hit the front for the first time.

The Hawks lifted, as champion teams always do. Robert 'Dipper' DiPierdomenico knocked out Kevin Walsh, and Peter Curran kicked a goal after Terry Daniher gave away a 15 metre penalty. But there were more signs that Hawthorn was tiring. Dipper got a cramp, and our plan to run him ragged started paying dividends at last. A shot at goal that he would normally have kicked was instead marked by Billy Duckworth, who set up a brilliant team goal that went the length of the field.

Duckworth kicked it to Bradbury, who kicked it to Roger Merrett, who brought the ball down and handballed it to Mark Harvey. He kicked it towards 'the Flying Dutchman', Paul Vander Haar, who knocked it to Paul Weston, who had by now been shifted forward, and he kicked the goal. Then Tim Watson kicked two more goals, and while Leigh Matthews got another for the Hawks, we answered with one from Merv Neagle. Someone shouted 'sound the siren please', and when it did go, it was magic – on the field, in the box, in the stands.

Essendon supporters celebrated their first premiership in nearly two decades, Billy Duckworth got the Norm Smith Medal and the coach was safe for at least another year. Lou Richards was one of the Channel Seven commentators that day, and he was generous in his praise after the game, saying that the decision to shift players around the field had contributed to the win. While that was gratifying to hear, make no mistake, it's players who win premierships, and all credit goes to them. ●

Great captain, Terry Daniher; he made everyone in the club happy. And Tim Watson was a great player, a superstar who the fans always came to see. You can also see legendary Colin Hooper there in the background, who ran the interchange for 20 years and has served in various roles at the club for over 40 years. That's the sort of dedication that makes clubs great.

BACK TO BACK IN 1985

WE WON ANOTHER GRAND FINAL IN 1985, AND probably won the fight that broke out at the start of the game. You did that back then, just to let the opposition know you were fair dinkum. With all the fines for melees these days no club could afford to do it now.

It was an incredible performance, and we won by 78 points. Simon Madden won the Norm Smith Medal for a dominant display. I said to the players afterwards, 'It took you five years to play four quarters of football, but I'm patient. It was a wonderful effort of football, the way football should be played.' It was a very proud moment.

Losing two grand finals in a row would have hurt Hawthorn. Years before, Allan Jeans and I had fallen out over what was meant to be a complimentary remark. After the drubbing Hawthorn gave us in the 1983 final, I said, 'Whatever they're on, we wouldn't mind some of it.' He thought it insinuated that the Hawks were taking drugs, and our relationship never recovered from that. He would have enjoyed us losing the elimination final to Fitzroy in 1986, leaving Hawthorn to beat Carlton in the grand final.

With a mesmerising voice and outstanding values, Allan Jeans was a great coach of a great team in his time at Hawthorn. We could be happy to have just snuck in a couple of premierships between all the ones the Hawks won during the 1980s. 🏉

The 1985 Grand Final parade. There wasn't much happiness in this photo between Allan Jeans and myself. Allan was a great coach and a respected rival, but off-field we got off on the wrong foot and our relationship never really recovered.

OPPOSITE: Allan Jeans is saying: 'Enjoy, son, they are very hard to win.' He never said much to me, so I remember this moment well.

ABOVE: Back to back premiership cups from 1984 and 1985, with Simon Madden and the man who'd recently replaced him as captain, Terry Daniher. Both these men played like leaders, so the captaincy is really only a name – if we're talking purely about leadership roles, there were probably eight captains in that Essendon team.

RIGHT: After the celebrations, you realise how tired you are at the end of the season. It's mentally exhausting and takes a long time to recover.

COACHING FOR THE COACH

ONE OF THE REASONS I WROTE *THE 500 CLUB* with Warwick Hadfield in 2004 was because when I came to Essendon as the first full-time coach in the VFL, there was no textbook. The information was out there – and when I say out there, not just in Victoria but all over the world – but no one had ever pulled it together. So we brought together all the ideas of David Parkin, Allan Jeans, Ron Barassi, Tom Hafey and Jock McHale in the one place.

When I first arrived at Essendon, I was very much a coach of the Richmond school, mainly the Tommy Hafey and Graeme Richmond school: supreme fitness, hard football and a hatred of losing. That helped get us to those premierships in 1984 and 1985. The players were a lot fitter by then; they had hardened up, and the complacency that marked the club when I first joined had gone.

With the luxury of a couple of premierships under my belt, I found time to go looking for

1988. There was a bit of media interest in the lead-up to my 200th game as coach. No one could have realised there was still such a long way to go.

other coaching ideas. In America, there was the great Vince Lombardi, coach of the Green Bay Packers, from whom to draw both inspiration and ideas. I was first introduced to him when Tom Hafey gave me one of his books.

I discovered that Lombardi had been influenced by other great coaches like Colonel Earl 'Red' Blaik from the West Point Military Academy, who was known for applying military discipline to the NFL. Then Lombardi worked as an assistant coach with another NFL legend: the highly creative Tom Landry. When these two were the assistants for the New York Giants, the senior coach Jim Lee Howell said all that was left for him to do was to make sure the balls had air in them. From that story, I might have learned that it is okay to delegate, something I wasn't that good at when I first arrived at Essendon.

By the time Lombardi became a head coach, he had collected a host of ideas to apply to his team. Under him, the Green Bay Packers – or the Cheeseheads as they were known – won the first two Superbowls and five NFL Championships.

One of Lombardi's strengths was being able to unite his players. He had suffered from racism because of his Italian background, and he hated it. He took a stand against racism in the NFL, insisting that all of them, regardless of colour, stay in the same hotel – to him 'everyone was green'. Even though he was a devout Catholic who went to Mass most days, he was also an early advocate for gay rights, recruiting gay players and threatening to sack anyone who didn't like the idea. He was not afraid to challenge the thinking of his time.

You should never be frightened to take ideas from any sport that might help you, no matter how far it might seem from your own game. There's plenty of information to mine: some of it might be technical aspects of a game that could translate well to Aussie Rules, and some might be about ways to grow your club and your game. That's why we went to Old Trafford in the late 1990s, and why I went again in 2013.

People accuse me of stealing ideas, but I don't, I only borrow them – and I always give them back ... eventually. I possibly repaid soccer, at least. On 28 October 2005 there were two big events planned for Melbourne: an International Rules game at one end of the city, and a Melbourne Victory match at the other end, and both were struggling with ticket sales. The AFL wanted me to get a bigger crowd for the International Rules, and the Victory CEO Geoff Miles and I had a conversation around what we might do to boost interest in his game too. →

Chasing knowledge in America. We visited the Atlanta Falcons in the early 80s. The recruiting network, the filming of every player and the incredible professionalism were the three main things I took from this trip and could implement immediately for success. You couldn't try more than three because, remember, this was a club who had just reluctantly forked out for a ball for each player!

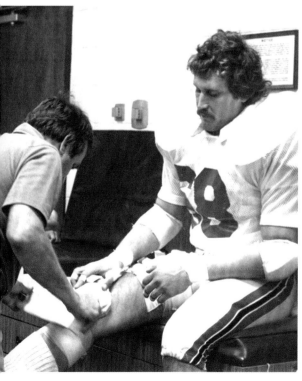

1989, against Geelong in the preliminary final at Waverly Park. Concentration is a tremendously important part of a coach's work. You have to keep your eyes on the job and show no emotion. I think the cameras are too intrusive these days. When that started happening, I tried to disappear up the back so the TV cameras couldn't find me.

Old Trafford, assistant coaches' tour, 1999. I got in trouble for wearing that Musashi hat everywhere I went, so I gave it to Harves for this photo. We had to fund the trip somehow, and a little bit of advertising provided what the club would not. It was around the time of Alex Ferguson's testimonial game, and was one of my greatest coaching trips ever. I've no doubt it contributed to a premiership in 2000.

At a press conference for International Rules, I asked a friend to wait until the media had finished, then ask me a question about how I felt going up against a soccer match. I said: 'Nil-all, 1-nil, 1-all, get a life.'

Suddenly both games were all over the back pages; talkback radio switchboards lit up like Christmas trees. Soccer people rang in to criticise me, footy people rang in to support me. We got a decent crowd in the end, and so did Victory. Geoff Miles and I shared a bottle of champagne to celebrate our success.

There should be healthy competition between sports, but that doesn't mean you have to isolate yourself. When you look outside the Melbourne bubble to discover great people like Lombardi, you find a treasure trove of ideas to rework and apply to what you're trying to do.

And they don't have to be football people, either. The best assistant coach I ever had was a bloke who never got paid a cent by either Essendon or the Giants: Edward de Bono, the inventor of the Lateral Thinking technique and Brain Training. Born in Malta, where he won a Rhodes Scholarship to attend Oxford, he would never have heard of Australian football. But when I was awarded the Thinker of the Year prize in 2008, he was one of the first people I thanked.

That title, Thinker of the Year, was a great honour, and a sign of how far I had come on my journey from back-pocket plumber, and how much I had been changed by all the wonderful people and ideas I discovered along the way. They're out there, you just have to go looking for them. 🏈

FIELDS OF DREAMS

LOU RICHARDS BEGAN CALLING ESSENDON'S HOME ground in Napier Street 'Windy Hill' back in the 1950s, which meant I probably should have realised well before becoming Essendon coach that the way the wind was blowing would determine how you play there. It was always windy at Windy Hill: a dirty wind that made up its own mind about which way it was going to blow. To make things worse for the visitors, the ground is not a true oval but shaped more like an egg.

At Richmond, I'd had no idea about any of this. When I got to Essendon, I started listening to all the old players: if the wind was coming through the two grandstands, you played down one wing. If it was coming from the outer end, you'd go the other way towards goal. At training and on match day, the windsock was a vital asset. Once we knew which way the wind was blowing we would do hours of monotonous circle work in the one area, just to make sure we had everything right on match day if the wind came from the same direction. If it didn't, well, we had already done monotonous hours of practice going the other way.

It was a real advantage for us to know which way the wind was blowing on match day (in the hope that the opposition didn't realise how to use it to their advantage), but it wasn't me who tied up the windsock when we played the West Coast at Windy Hill in 1991 – though Mick Malthouse thought it

was. He'd had plenty of experience playing with the wind during his time as coach of Footscray. I saw players cringe before running out into the wind and wet at Whitten Oval, as it is now called, saying to each other, 'Surely they aren't going to make us go out and play in that!'

You had to have different strategies for all the different suburban grounds in Melbourne, with each team trying to get a home ground advantage. Since 1965, Richmond's home ground had been the MCG: my field of dreams. But some of the other grounds around Melbourne back then were fields of nightmares. When Allan Jeans was coach of St Kilda, he liked his players to be running around on a wet track at Moorabbin. If it hadn't rained for a while, you needed to keep an eye out for fire hoses. At Lakeside, when the wind was coming off the beach and the lake – often at the same time – you had to be very careful with your kicking.

When you go past Glenferrie Oval now on the train out to Belgrave, it's hard to believe that we used to play VFL football there, and that in 1965 they got nearly 36,000 people to a game between the Hawks and Carlton. It is so small that we used to call it 'the sardine tin' – that's when it wasn't being called 'the gluepot' because the drainage was so poor. It would take days to get all the mud off after playing there. Most school grounds now are better than Glenferrie Oval used to be.

Essendon's beloved Windy Hill is shaped more like an egg than an oval. Luckily for us, the famous wind played havoc with our opponents. Hasn't scoreboard advertising changed since then? I love these photos – every one tells a story.

The occupational health and safety rules that we have today would have prevented us from playing in those conditions. I remember when Mark Harvey came back to coach at Essendon, and he was amazed to see us call off training because of a thunder storm. He reckoned that in his playing days I would have made him and rest of his teammates stay out there – apparently I'd 'gone soft'. But by then it was a workplace safety issue. Imagine how hard Workcover would come down on you if one of your players got struck by lightning.

These days I think we're all grateful we have just two AFL grounds in Melbourne, and both are coliseums with lush, dry playing surfaces. At the MCG you don't have to worry too much about the wind or the mud, and thanks to the roof at Docklands you aren't even troubled by lightning. Pretty much all the grounds around Australia are coliseums, or soon will be.

I like watching the way our grounds have changed over the years. I took a personal interest in the development of Spotless Stadium in Sydney, photographing it on an almost daily basis as it took shape. The new Adelaide Oval, which still has its scoreboard hill to let a bit of wind in, is a brilliant asset for football and cricket, and while Kardinia Park still has the Gary Ablett Terrace, it is otherwise now pretty much surrounded by stands. At Metricon, well, it is always beautiful one day, perfect the next – it is in Queensland, after all. Perth's new stadium, a mini MCG that holds 60,000 people, will be a coliseum too.

Speaking of the Gary Ablett outer, I am reminded of the story of Daryl Somers, the host of *Hey Hey It's Saturday* and a former number-one ticket holder with Geelong. When he was a boy standing in that outer, he couldn't see the football over the crowd, so he'd wait until his father had drunk four cans of beer, then use the empties as stilts to let him get a view of the game. That's just another sign of how much football, watching it and playing it, has changed in my time. A lot of people don't like change, but I don't think in 2017, when you look back at the sardine can, or the egg-shape or the four-beer-can stand, anyone has any real grounds of complaint. 🏉

OPPOSITE: Over the years I've coached and played over 250 games at the MCG, the home of footy. I feel very comfortable here.

ABOVE: In the early days of the Giants, Dave Matthews made the decision to buy a driving range, and we built a stadium called Spotless. Every day after training I'd go and take photos. We also rescued Manuka Oval in Canberra and entered a partnership with the ACT Government to put some loyalty back into that city, which had felt overlooked by Melbourne clubs in the past. Tom Wills, creator of Australian Rules, lived in the Molonglo Plain, and he deserves a team in his own backyard.

Great players coached and coached against.

OPPOSITE: Darren Millane. Wouldn't you love to have him in your side? Much of the difference between Essendon and Collingwood in the 1990 Grand Final was Millane's spirit and courage – even though it erupted in a brawl.

ABOVE: 'Michael, put some weight on. Geez, Michael, I didn't mean so much!' By 2000 Michael Long was able to take out a 6 foot 5 ruckman with a bump (it cost him a few weeks, though).

LEFT: Terry Wallace, Peter Daicos and myself – obviously Daicos and Wallace didn't really feel like training for the Victorian side.

The greatest promoter the game has ever known

Kevin Sheedy is an adventurer, and one of his biggest adventures began when he joined Essendon and became the first person in footy to be full-time on purpose. There were others who had to put in full-time hours, but that was only because they weren't properly organised.

Kevin wasn't the only person considered for the coaching position at Essendon. There were rumours that I might get the job, but that was never going to happen because I had plans to go back to Melbourne, the place I call home. Allan Jeans was also considered, but in the end Kevin was selected.

I coached against Kevin at Melbourne and later when I was with the Swans, and I can tell you the hardest working person in the coach's box when you played Essendon was the bloke moving the magnets – your board man. That's because Kevin was always making lots of unusual moves, probably too many moves, but I am not one to really criticise other coaches, particularly when you don't know what led them to make the moves they did.

On match day, the pressure is on, you've got to make decisions and make them fast. Sometimes you move one player instead of another. At the time of making that decision you're almost 50/50 – say 51/49 – that it's the right decision. If it turns out that you were wrong, well, you weren't *that* far wrong.

Great coaching is all about making great decisions. Rarely can you do that with the luxury of time, rather, it's fractions of a second stuff. Kevin Sheedy proved himself to be a great coach – there is no doubt about

that. It's not just because he had four premierships during his 27 years coaching Essendon: being a good coach is about more than just winning premierships. Len Smith, the brother of Norm Smith, who coached me at Melbourne, won no premierships, but he is regarded as a great coach.

Kevin made a bit of a rod for himself on the way to becoming a great coach by taking on the additional role of being a super-salesman for football and for his clubs. That's an awful lot of extra work you must do in the media, travelling the country, as Kevin did, to tell anyone who'll listen about what a great game Australian Rules Football is. And to add to the workload, he took his team with him too. When he was at Essendon, they used to call him the Paladin – 'Have Team, Will Travel', after the western cowboy known as Paladin whose motto was, 'Have Gun, Will Travel'.

Kevin has had amazing success in that role, as well as becoming a great coach. He was and still is the best promoter the game has ever seen. It is obvious in just about everything he does that he has the deepest of love for Australian football. He's not the sort of person to fall into the trap of working at something he doesn't like. I don't think I marketed the game at the same level that Kevin does. I probably didn't think about it as deeply as Kevin. That might be because until 1993, when I went to Sydney to coach the Swans, I had never been a full-time coach, but Kevin was marketing the game even before he became a full-time coach, working as a development officer while he was still at Richmond. He was already travelling then, to Tasmania and into schools around Victoria, so it seems he always had this need to promote the game.

Kevin's records, the premierships, the sheer longevity of his coaching career, all tell you he is very good at making the right decisions – and many times, great decisions. He's also been very good at keeping his clubs growing, both on and off the field. Essendon's huge membership now can be traced straight back to what he did when he was coach, and what he has done since returning to the club. Having coached in Sydney, I know how hard that market is to crack, but look at what

he did for Greater Western Sydney while he was there.

It's all down to the thought he puts into promoting both the clubs he is coaching and the game. He was very good at getting the balance right between having a good team each season, as well as building for the seasons ahead, keeping the supporters happy and keeping the membership growing. There's no doubt about it – Kevin Sheedy remains to this day unique in Australian football.

Ron Barassi AM, AFL Hall of Fame Legend.

Barassi was a genius coach, and he took both North Melbourne and Carlton to the heights they'd been seeking before he was appointed. I loved watching him his whole career; he was always thinking smarter and better than most people. This photo features two legends eyeballing each other: Barassi and Blight.

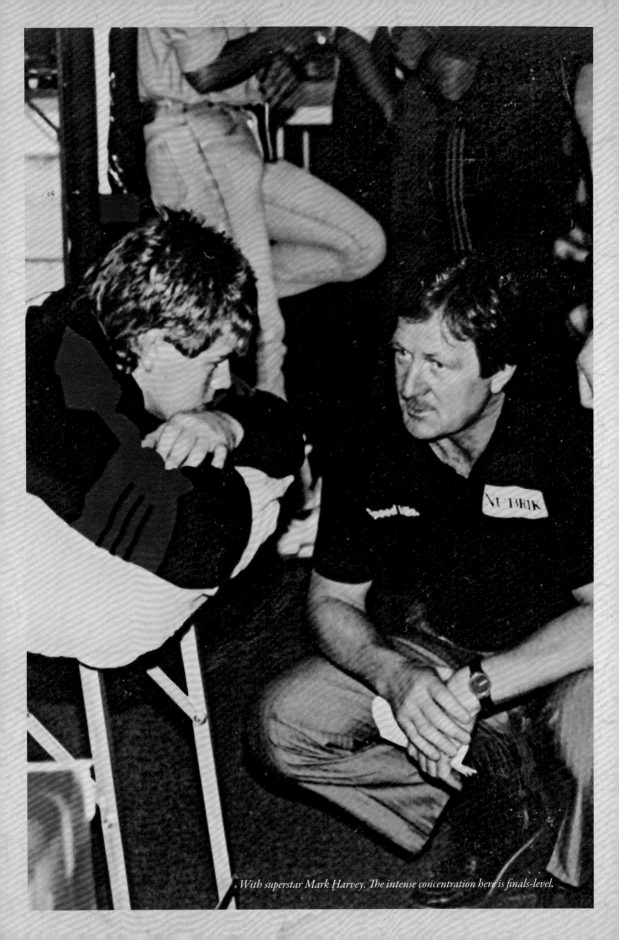

With superstar Mark Harvey. The intense concentration here is finals-level.

6

THE 1990S

We had our ups and downs in the 90s, but it was an era in which many fine people, true club legends, embedded the deep and abiding Bomber culture that has benefitted us ever since.

You could say I'm a bit of a hoarder. Before everything went electronic I had a huge video library – all football matches and motivating movies of sportspeople and world greats. I'd study videos of opposition teams, and at the same time I'd check the reports on these games in the papers to see how they were interpreting and judging matches. Chase knowledge and share it.

Kevin Sheedy

1990 – AN UNWELCOME BREAK

SOME PEOPLE SAY THAT PETER SUMICH LOST US the 1990 Grand Final. We won 17 games that season (the first of the 'AFL') and were the minor premiers, which gave us the first week of the finals off. On Saturday 8 September – the date is etched in my mind – we went out to Waverley to watch West Coast play Collingwood in a qualifying final. The match was in the balance right up until the end when, with 30 seconds to go and Collingwood ahead by a point, Peter took a mark in the forward pocket.

A goal would have changed history. Instead the kick across the face of the goal made us history. The draw meant the match had to be replayed the following week. So instead of one week off for us, it was now two, and in the case of some of the players, it would be three. To get all four Daniher brothers a game together, in the final home and away round, we had rested some of our senior players. That break was a disaster.

Confidence, momentum, form: in footy they come and go on a whim. They don't need three weeks to plan their departure. Certainly, all three had checked out by the time we finally made our way to the MCG for the second semi-final against Leigh Matthews's Pies, who were battle-hardened by all their extra footy.

Just like the Bulldogs in 2016, they kept on playing and kept on winning.

The following week, we got some revenge on Peter Sumich by beating the Eagles in the preliminary final, but in the grand final, once again, confidence, momentum and form never showed up. We shouldn't have let it happen, but we did – players, coaches, everyone was to blame, along with bloody Peter Sumich. It was a thrashing. Question: Who kicked five goals in the 1990 Grand Final? Answer: Essendon.

But there was one important difference between the Essendon of a decade before and the Essendon of 1990: the players were gutted. Tim Watson wrote, 'At times like this, you only feel contempt for the game.'

You don't always win, and as a coach, you have to learn to cope with losing even if you don't want to – and teach your players how to do it too. You have to stress the importance to them of why you lost and what you can learn.

Up, up and away with the Danihers

I remember Kevin desperately wanted all four Daniher brothers – Terry, Neale, Anthony and Chris – to play together for Essendon. This meant a lot of travel up to the Danihers' 5000-acre family farm at Ungarie in New South Wales, where the Daniher boys and their seven sisters grew up under the knowing gaze of Jim and Edna.

Jim was a good sportsman himself. He played Australian Rules football and representative Rugby League, so obviously it was in the genes, as we can see now with Joe Daniher. One time, to make it easier for everyone to get to Ungarie, football manager Kevin Egan, who was training to be a pilot, arranged for us to fly there. We arrived to discover that there was a runway of sorts on the farm, but no con-trol tower, so the pilot used a tree as the marker when he came in to land.

We spent the day in the company of Jim and Edna Daniher and the boys, playing cricket rather than football. When it came time to fly home, the pilot told us he was a bit worried because without a control tower or even a windsock, he couldn't work out the wind direction. With a sort of 'you're in the country now' look on his face, Jim Daniher licked his finger, held it up to the breeze and declared the wind was coming from the north-east. When we were in the air, the pilot turned around to tell us Jim had been right.

Everyone was relieved to be heading safely home, but that changed in an instant when the door next to Kevin flew

open and he let out an almighty shout. Fortunately, he was strapped in, but that didn't stop him from trying to close the door with a look of fear on his face that got bigger and bigger as he realised he wasn't strong enough to close it, even though by now he was using a second seat belt that he had attached to the door to try to pull it in.

Kevin didn't get much sympathy from the rest of us. The pilot told him not to worry – he wouldn't fall out, and anyway, as Jim Daniher had already pointed out, the wind was coming from the other direction. I was even less supportive, saying to him, 'This is football, Kevin, the coach always goes before the committee.' As it turns out, he outlasted everyone who was at Essendon when he joined.

Neville Gay, long-time Essendon committeeman and a member of the panel that employed Kevin at Essendon.

OPPOSITE: By the end of 1981, when I made him captain, Neale Daniher had already had three knee recos. Talk about a recovery! He's gone on to an excellent coaching career, including being the last coach to take Melbourne to a grand final. The decision to get rid of him at Melbourne was a devastating one, but the decision not to have him replace me at Essendon was even more ridiculous.

RIGHT (TOP and BOTTOM): Taking the plunge. Neale Daniher has done amazing work raising awareness and money for motor neurone disease research. My granddaughter, Charlotte, asked me to participate dressed as Tinkerbell – the things you do for your grandkids.

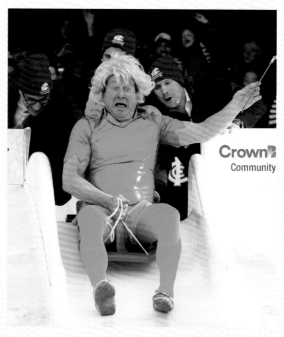

Terry Daniher in 1984, the super captain. In an interview with Terry, the ABC's Norman May was bemused by the idea of a New South Welshman playing Australian Rules rather than rugby. What he didn't know was all four Daniher brothers had played Rugby League as well as AFL. The rugby talent scouts had their chance, we just beat them to it!

What goes on in that brain?

'Christ, you look like the kind of girl I used to date in the 1960s!' They were the first words Kevin Sheedy spoke to me – an interesting start if ever there was one to what has been a great friendship. It was in 1999 at the Hyatt where, for the first time, I was to be the moderator of the Essendon Women's Network Grand Final Comedy Debate, to give it its full name, and I was wearing a red dress with sequins and had a feather boa in red and black, as you do when you barrack for the Bombers.

Kevin was a big part of that debate. He was very funny, and you could tell he just loved the event because he'd always rec-ognised the value of female fans of football, who are about 45 to 50 per cent of footy audiences, and who are just as passionate about the game as anyone else. I ended up doing about ten of those debates after originally being roped in by Joan Kirner, the former Victorian premier, to go to a Women's Network event. I think I was set up, because I walked in the door and Linda Dessau, who is now the Governor of Victo-ria, took me aside and said, 'I hear you want to help us on the committee.' Why wouldn't you want to work with good people like Joan, Linda, Joanne Albert and Di Gribble, who were also some of the original mem-bers of the network? They had gone to Kevin and said there should be a women's network, and he embraced and supported us in everything we did.

I won a signed football in a raffle one year. At the end of the event, Kevin an-nounced that everyone who had won a prize in the raffle that day could have their photo taken with the Essendon team. A couple

Geeze, photo quality has improved, hasn't it? Rock'n'Roll night at Essendon. If I wasn't into footy, I would have been in a band – I feel better on a microphone these days. Always had great times with our coteries at Essendon.

of weeks later I went out to Windy Hill and there were around 100 people in the rooms waiting for their team photograph. I was thinking, how is this possibly going to work? It was a lovely gesture – the sort of thing he always does to promote the club – but are all of us going to be in the picture?

Then we were all given a number and in came the players from training. They set up like they normally would for a team photo but left a gap in the middle, and everyone took it in turns to sit in the gap and have their photo taken. When my number was called out I had James Hird on one side and Matthew Lloyd on the other and Kevin had his arm around me. Have I died and gone to heaven? They took two photos. For the first one it was 'everyone smile', and for the second one it was with the team cheering. Kevin was the one leading the cheering every time. The players were just fantastic, and they did it 100 times without any grumbling. I guess they knew it was Kevin building another bond between the club and the supporters. A few weeks later the photo arrived and it was huge, a photo that you treasure forever. It is still up on the wall of my office.

After another debate at Crown, I was sitting with my partner, Paul, and Kevin having a drink and, well, I always had a thing about Aaron Henneman – like why is he picked, how does he get a game? It was a bit of a cheek really since I don't know a lot about football and Kevin Sheedy does; I asked him, why do you pick

Aaron Henneman? And he answered with a mathematical formula: Aaron Henneman is a 6, and Mark Johnson is a 12, and Danny Jacobs is a 4.7. The way he justified Aaron Henneman in the team was a mathematical formula! I am just thinking to myself, 'What goes on in your brain?'

It is just such a phenomenal brain, and I found it heartbreaking the way he was dismissed from the club – that was so disrespectful of what he had done. He should have been allowed to go when he wanted to, but typical of Kevin, he saw it as an opportunity – look what he did with the Giants. And anyway, he's back now.

That's another thing I like about Kevin: he is always big on opportunity – that and the fact that he can always make me laugh, as he did that first time we met and he reminded me – not that I needed it – that I was a child of 60s. Thanks for that, Kev!

Jane Clifton, actor, singer, author and Essendon supporter.

We'd often bring the fanbase and members in for special shots, and we'd keep the team posed there for half an hour. It meant that those who contributed to the club – coterie, lifetime members – had something special to keep. The money raised from these photoshoots also helped the team go overseas and chase knowledge that would grow the club further.

RETURN TO FORM

N MANY WAYS, THAT LOSS IN 1990 LAID THE foundation for 1993, the year of the Bombers. We won everything: the night premiership, the Michael Tuck Medal, the minor premiership, the Brownlow Medal, the Norm Smith Medal, the Jock McHale Medal and the flag. To top it all off, Tim Watson was named Victorian Father of the Year!

Mention of Tim reminds me of how close we came to missing out on the 1993 flag. Tim had retired at the end of the 1991 season, but we had talked him into another year in 1993. We got to the preliminary final against Adelaide but trailed by 42 points at half-time. I was angry, but not with the players. As the coaches had made their way to the rooms, we had seen Graham Cornes, the Adelaide coach, with his feet up on the desk and a look on his face that said, 'How easy is this?' You don't disrespect a club like Essendon that way.

When we got to the rooms, I walked among the players, talking softly, reminding them they were on this great journey of a footballing life and that there would be times when they would have to go deeper into themselves than they ever thought possible. Now was one of those times. Here was not a threat, but an opportunity to do something that would give them a special place in the history of their club and their game and make everyone proud of them.

A video still from a very happy moment. This game put us on top of AFL in 1993, but the jacket wave is remembered more than the game. The young people are laughing, but the elderly gentleman on my right isn't so sure. My superstar Computer Recruiting Programmer Anthony Northwood (the man on the right with the sideburns) also seems to be enjoying it. He worked for me for ten years, collating information – a mad Bomber fan.

You didn't need to tell Tim Watson that. He had done it many times, but could he do it one more time? 'Tim, is this how you want it all to end?' I asked. 'Do you want your whole career to end like this? This might be the last match in your last season, your last 60 minutes of football. Do you want to go out there and end it all? Do you want to look back on your career and know it ended in defeat – that you never played in a last grand final you might have been in?'

> What followed was an amazing turnaround, and history has recorded that Tim Watson kicked the final goal in a famous Essendon win. But according to Adelaide mid-fielder Mark Bickley, someone farting was the reason the Crows lost focus.

Many years after the game, he revealed that Greg Anderson, a former Essendon player who had joined the Crows and was working for Musashi, had all these powders and mixtures that played havoc with everyone's stomachs. At the end of the half-time break, Cornes pulled all the team into a close group and 'someone farted while he was trying to be serious and deliver this great speech, and everyone was holding their nose'. It's an ill wind that blows no good.

There have been bigger comebacks in the history of our game (and the Bombers coming back to beat North at the MCG in

2001, after being 10 goals down at quarter-time, was probably the best game I was ever involved in) but few felt better than this one in 1993, particularly with a place in the grand final up for grabs. The final score was 17.9 (111) to 14.16 (100).

It seems strange to say, but the grand final the next week was almost an anticlimax. We had winners all over the ground. Michael Long was harder to catch than a zephyr; Gavin Wanganeen proved that winning the Brownlow hadn't affected his focus; the Marks, Thompson and Harvey were absolute

rocks down back; Sean Denham stayed attached to Greg Williams like a shadow and Gary O'Donnel fought it out with Long for the Norm Smith Medal. And there were James Hird and Mark Mercuri, the kids we had decided to play at the start of the season. We tanked a premiership in 1993. Tanks for the memories.

Mark Thompson was an obvious choice as captain when his time came because he was already running his own electrical business and employing lots of different characters. He later proved he could lead a club as well as a team when he became coach of Geelong, helping restore the faith of Cats supporters with two premierships after they had lost those four grand finals in 1989, 1992, 1994 and 1995 and the club had almost gone broke.

There were other highlights, and lowlights, in the rest of the 1990s. James Hird shared a Brownlow with Michael Voss in 1996, but Carlton got a good measure of revenge for 1993 in the 1999 preliminary final, beating us by a point. By now there had been a few people working against me as coach. We needed another flag, and soon.

GAMES RECORD

IT WAS ALWAYS A PLEASURE TO SIT AND HAVE A cup of tea with Dick Reynold, the King of Windy Hill, who took the Bombers to four premierships as a captain–coach.

I'm glad Brian Donohoe talked me out of being a player–coach myself. Brian said I was too old, but I suspect he just thought it was a bad idea. I had tried player–coaching in the Army and knew how hard it was to organise your teammates while still concentrating on your own game. Dick had been brilliant at it, though. He coached Essendon in 415 games, and going past that record in round 16 in 1998 was something about which I felt very proud.

Another person I'd have loved to have a cup of tea with is the ghost of coaching who sits above us all: Collingwood's Jock McHale. He won premierships as a captain–coach and as a coach across 714 games.

Mick Malthouse has gone past Jock's record for most games as coach, and I've gone past his record for most games as a player and coach, but with a career that lasted from 1903 to 1949, he's still an imposing figure. I would like to ask him where he got the energy to keep going so long. Maybe he would ask me the same question, and I suspect our answers would match: 'I just love the game.'

Over my career I totalled 929 games as player and coach. That's a lot of training sessions and games for the few hours of happiness you get when you win a grand final, but I'd have to say it was worth it. 🏉

Another fun day in the job. Most people think it's actually Robin Williams in this photo – Billy Brownless has always called me Robin Williams.

Player revolt

When Kevin Sheedy first came to Essen-don, word spread that there would be some blood-letting and he would be bringing all his ideas from Richmond on how to make the Bombers more professional. One of the first things he did was to have all these signs made up saying, 'Players, Officials and Staff Only'. I had already been 'access all areas' for a while, thanks to Kevin's predecessors Barry Davis and Bill Stephen.

When the time came for the first meeting between Kevin and the players, I took up my usual place in the room. 'What are you doing here?' said Kevin.

'I am part of the furniture', I said.

'No way get him out of here!' Sheeds yelled.

Well, that sparked a players' revolt. Simon Madden, Garry Foulds, Steve Taubert – there was quite a number of them – they all said, 'If The Phantom goes, we all go.' A couple of days later, Kevin called me into his office and told me he was going to keep me on, and from there came a wonderful friendship. I've held a lot of jobs at the club, including attending match committee meeting as chairman of the non-selection panel. I've shared a lot of opinions with him on which players to pick. I think we even share the same political views; I appointed him secretary of the Essendon Football Club branch of the plumbers' union, and we went around calling each other 'comrade'.

There was a time I might have strained the friendship a bit. It was a match com-mittee meeting with Sheeds, Kevin Egan, Mark Harvey, Robert Shaw and football manager Danny Corcoran. They had ordered fish and chips for the end of the meeting, but I ate them before it finished. There was a bit of a hiatus after that, but not for long.

The 1984 and 1985 premierships were two of the most marvellous days of my life. They were a special group of people who won those flags, particularly Simon Madden and Mark Harvey. There's another day from around that time, in 1986, that's memorable for all the wrong reasons – it was the dreadful moment when Micky Conlan kicked a goal to give Fitzroy a one-point win over Essendon in the elimination final at Waverley.

I went up to the club on the Monday after the game and I met Kevin, who was about to have a meeting with the players in the Andrew Peacock room at Windy Hill. He said I had better come along. Let me tell you, he was angry, so I left after about 10 minutes. I thought I'd better get out while I was still in one piece, and as I was walking down the street I could still hear Sheeds going off his head. He was angry with all the players – he had a go at Simon Madden, but he reserved something special for Michael Thomson: 'You will never play for Essendon again, you're finished.' Michael Thomson had done a pretty good job on Micky Conlan all day, it was just in those last few minutes of the game that he left him unmarked. In 1987, he was granted a clearance to Richmond.

The Phantom: the real coach of Essendon. If anybody deserves a photograph with four premiership cups, it's him. His morale-boosting speeches were the finest I have ever seen in my life. He would give it to every superstar and the coach if he didn't think you were performing. I've seen Watson, Madden, Daniher, Lloyd and Hird all get strips torn off them, piece by piece. The press couldn't do it, but The Phantom could. 'You better be on this week,' he'd say, 'this is the mountaintop!'

The 2000 premiership was another special moment for me. The players had requested that I be allowed down on the ground at the end of the game. At three-quarter time, I went down and sat with Col Hooper, one of the trainers. The coaches' boxes were just to our left, and me being 'access all areas', I managed to get close, and it became my job to call the players off. I called Hirdie off, and John Barnes, but he didn't want to come. That was a very special experience, standing there with the boys, watching them get their medals, then going into the room to sing the song, where I got wet with champagne.

One of the saddest days, though, was when I went up to see Sheeds and James Hird in the week leading up to their last game for Essendon in 2007, against Richmond. I had bought each of them flowers – lilies – to say thanks for all they had done for the club, and for me. I chose flowers because I know Kevin loves his garden and I knew James would appreciate that too. I went to Kevin's office and gave him his flowers, and he had tears in his eyes. Then I went to see James, and we cried together.

It's great that Kevin is back at Essendon again. He's a marvellous friend, a great character. He treats everyone the same, regardless of their religion, the colour of their skin or if they have a disability.

Mark 'The Phantom' Doran, Essendon Football Club's Chairman of the Non-Selection Panel.

POLITICAL GAMES

AROUND THE LATE 1990S, WHAT JAMES HIRD has called 'the putsch' was on to get rid of me as coach of Essendon. Word spread that my place there was uncertain, and in 1999 my old club, Richmond, came a calling, asking me to come 'home' as coach. Quite a few clubs had been making contact, but Richmond was the one that was the hardest to resist, because I love both Essendon and Richmond equally. It had got to the stage where the negotiations with Essendon for a new contract were going nowhere and Richmond was in front.

Close friends of mine were told of a press conference to be held after the last home-and-away game against Melbourne to announce a move to Richmond, but one of them, Lionel Krongold, a member of the Essendonians coterie, wouldn't hear of it. He reminded me that at the time Richmond was a club with financial issues, and that the Bombers were a lot closer to a premiership than the Tigers. He also spoke to the president and CEO, Graham McMahon and Peter Jackson, and in the end, there was a press conference … to announce that the coach had re-signed at Essendon for another three years.

It wasn't just Lionel Krongold helping me out around that time. After I'd chosen one week to go and watch a player we were thinking of recruiting instead of next week's opponent, as coaches normally do, a newspaper ran a telephone poll about whether it was the right move by Essendon's senior coach. Brian Donohoe hit the re-dial button on his phone enough times for the poll to end up 86-14 – in my favour.

But James Hird in particular should get a lot of the credit for me becoming a four-time premiership coach at Essendon. As the Bombers' newly appointed captain, he told officials that as far as he was concerned I had coached the club well for a long time and he didn't want to hear any more about the matter. Then there was the way James led the team so brilliantly after the shattering disappointment of the 1999 preliminary final against Carlton. It was on his insistence that all the players were to watch the grand final as a group, in their Essendon blazers, in the knowledge they should have been out in the middle instead of sitting in the grandstands. 🏉

During the 1999 preliminary final loss to Hawthorn. Not a happy little soul. I just had to keep concentrating on who'd done well and who had to lift in future big games.

Attack-minded to a fault

When I was coaching Carlton, Kevin Sheedy became the opposition coach I admired and feared most. In the 1990s Essendon had a 14-game winning run against the Blues, something that became a mental nightmare for us. In many of these losing games we would get in front, but Sheeds would produce something totally out of left field, which we, the players and the coach, failed to deal with.

In the finish, we were prepared to do anything to stop their domination! Our coaching panel devised a strategy – not very legal or in the spirit of our great game – to stop the rot. To upset the Bombers, we would start a fight at the beginning of the game. Which means I do owe Kevin an apology: he got the blame for it. It was at Princes Park. We had our six forwards all stand around the boundary line at the first bounce. I said to my blokes, 'We've got to do something different; I want you to wrestle your man. We'll start six little fights.' It was the forwards against backs. Usually it is the other way around. We won the game and all the commentators and Carlton supporters were saying that the Bombers got their just desserts for starting the blue. Interestingly too, it started a nine-game run of successive victories for Carlton against the Bombers.

The great thing I always knew about Kevin as a coach was that when you were in front, if you thought you had him, you'd want to start to get very nervous because he would then produce something different. We'd spend a lot of time, as much as three hours, on our 'what ifs?' when preparing for a game against Essendon. More often than not, we still wouldn't guess what he would produce if we were in control of the game, or even before the start of the game – look at Derek Kickett in the 1993 Grand Final.

That element of surprise was his strength. I was methodical and took great pride in always being well-prepared. That made me easy to coach against, because the opposition knew how we would play. I'd just hope my players would be stronger than theirs. I was a defensive coach, the opposite of Kevin. But you could sometimes take advantage of his attacking approach.

> He had this Achilles heel that we can laugh about now. When he had outwitted you, he couldn't leave it alone. He had to see if he could do something even better, and it didn't always come off. So we were very nervous when we were in front, but there was always a chance when he was in front.

For Sheeds to stay at one club, one institution, for 27 years as he did at Essendon was just phenomenal. There are those who reckon he should have had more success with the Bombers. People who make those comments don't understand the modern structure of AFL football, which, with the draft and the salary cap, is now designed to have you win it every 18 years – with the addition of the Gold Coast and the Giants to the competition. Sheeds won four in 27 years at Essendon – one every seven years. That makes him a genius. In the future, people will look at his record and wonder how he was able to achieve it.

At the same time as he's delivered great performances, and brought teams together, and reinvented himself in terms of the team, he's promoted the Essendon Football Club – and then Greater Western Sydney – better than any coach has promoted any club. On top of that, he has a real issue about coaches being custodians of the game. I know he believes that deeply, so I dip my lid to him. I had other things in my life. I had another job, and I suppose if I had been a full-time coach I could have done these other things.

Like Sheeds, Ronald Dale Barassi is clearly Mr Football for the way he accepted he was just as responsible for the promotion of the game as he was for his own club. That's something I couldn't do; I was so involved in getting the coaching part of it right, and I didn't really see myself as an ambassador for the game. I got better at that at the finish. I probably learned some of that from Kevin too.

David Parkin OAM, premiership player and coach.

We always maintained that Essendon's colours were black with red, not red with black. Black always had to be the dominant colour on all team merchandise.

7

THE 2000S

We could not have started the noughties off in better style,
but I think the end could have been handled better.

'Mitchell White, you're dead!' I got the wrong information and behaved inappropriately at half-time against the Eagles in 2000. These photos capture the moment that I got fined $7500 for touching myself – it has to be some sort of world record.

THE MILLENNIUM WIN

HELPED ALONG THE WAY BY JAMES, LIONEL, GRAHAM McMahon and Brian, I was still Essendon coach going into the new millennium, and in the year the Olympics came back to Australia, the Bombers had their own gold medal moments. James Hird won the Norm Smith Medal, as much a reward for his leadership over the 12 months since the 1999 preliminary final as for his performance on the day.

The 2000 preliminary final presented more than a football challenge for James when his daughter Stephanie became seriously ill in the week leading up to the game. Sitting with James and his wife, Tania, in the hospital, I assured him that if he didn't want to play he didn't have to, that there are things more important than football. In the end he decided to play, and none of us took that decision for granted. Thankfully Stephanie made a complete recovery and these days is a beautiful and healthy young woman.

There is a beauty about the 2000 season that Bomber fans can reflect on forever. We won the minor premiership by 20 points, losing just one game for the season to the Bulldogs in Round 21. That was the day of the biggest flood since Noah, and a brawl at half-time that wasn't bad either. Some people said it was the game we needed to lose. Some people say some stupid things, but from there on we didn't miss a beat. We beat Collingwood in Round 22 by three goals, we thrashed the Kangaroos by 20 goals in the qualifying finals, Carlton by seven goals in the preliminary final (sweet revenge) and then in the grand final it was 10 goals over Melbourne, coached by Neale Daniher.

Paul Barnard and Matthew Lloyd, the Coleman Medallist, kicked four goals each. How lucky were we to have Lloyd and Scott Lucas, born just months apart, at Essendon at the same time? Some 1397 goals and not one handball between them (Scott Lucas will insist he handballed a lot more than Lloydie did). In 2000 John Barnes finally got a flag after playing in all those losing grand finals at Geelong. Like life, football is all about taking your opportunities, especially when they might be your last.

John Barnes's career was on the scrapheap in 1999 before we decided to give him a chance. When he arrived at Windy Hill he was as driven as any of the players who had lost that preliminary final. He could leap in the ruck and he could kick a few goals, so despite him being a different sort of bloke – he once called a media conference to say he was no longer talking to the media – we took him on. Barnsie is a good Essendon person – still a pest, but a good bloke.

Over 80,000 spectators turned up to watch us play West Coast in 2000 – many of them to wave their jackets. It's funny how an impulsive moment can create a fun tradition for people. A whole quarter of a century later they're still waving jackets.

ABOVE: My brother Bernard came to help us celebrate the premiership. My dad named each of his sons after one of the Catholic schools in Melbourne. Unfortunately he named me after one stuck in Toorak.

OPPOSITE: The marvellous Matthew Lloyd, one of the most professional players of all time. One of my biggest mistakes was not finding a way to award him a Best and Fairest – a man who kicked 926 goals. It makes me think of Michael Tuck, a player I always admired from a distance, and who never quite got the credit he deserved. Tuck played in seven Hawthorn premiership wins, four of which he captained. He kept going until he was 38, had 426 games, kicked 320 goals, but like Lloyd he never won a Best and Fairest. Not making it happen for Lloyd is a big regret of mine.

Adam Ramanauskas was the youngest member of the side, destined at 19 to be as good as Mark Mercuri and Michael Long, until he was diagnosed with cancer. For him to get back from that and play league footy again, well it's one of the great stories in the game. He's remarkable not just for his recovery, but for the way he went about it. Even while undergoing treatment, Adam was always thinking of his teammates in that selfless way of his, and they were always thinking about him, putting his number nine jumper at the top of the race and touching it as they ran out on to the field. 🏉

My last premiership, and the start of a new millennium.

James Hird at Windy Hill, celebrating his win of best-on-ground in the 2000 Grand Final – no wonder he's smiling. True Essendon fans still believe that Windy Hill is our home. It's an amazing place that's close to the hearts of many players, spectators and fans who have spent decades there. I wonder where they'll celebrate after the next premiership?

Getting me fired up

When I was in hospital for my first opera-tion after being diagnosed with cancer, everyone came in to see me – the players, the staff, the other coaches – but not Kevin, and I found that odd. On the day I was checking out, Essendon was playing the Bulldogs and no one had come to visit. The hospital was a ghost town, which was fair enough – they were all preparing for the game. Then suddenly out of nowhere and dressed in his full Essendon match-day gear, in comes Kevin, and he wants to talk to me about the game, which we did for about an hour.

I realised that was his way to keep me involved and to make me feel like I was part of the team. When I was first diagnosed, he asked me what I wanted to do, and I told him I wanted to be involved in the club and I wanted to be treated like everyone else, and he suggested that I become part of the coaching staff and that I mentor some of the younger players. That was a great experience for me because I was still pretty young myself, so it really helped me develop as a footballer and prepare for the time I got back to the game.

Those roles helped me to cope with all that I was going through; I could feel normal at the football club, and Kevin was the driver of all that. He has this hard exterior but he is a massive softie at heart, and he genuinely cares for all his players. What he did for Dean Rioli is another example of that: Kevin wanted him to get to 100 games, and it wasn't just about the father-son rule or anything like that, it was for Dean to have the achievement of having his name and 100 games written on his locker at Essendon.

I was the youngest member of the team that won the 2000 Grand Final, and people might think, how easy is that? You come into a club and you're a premiership player in a couple of years. But people don't realise how hard he made me work to get that spot. In 1999 Mark McVeigh and I were walking into Windy Hill together, and Kevin made a point of telling Mark in front of me that he would be playing his first game that week and obviously I wasn't. I am sure it was a tactic to make me want to work harder, and it worked – it really fired me up.

I played every game in 2000 and felt like I was a major contributor, though Kevin constantly kept me on my toes. After each game, he would critique my game strongly. I liked that, and he knew that's how I wanted it. As he did with other players, he just knew how to press my buttons. Some players might not know he was doing that, but I did and it was not dissimilar to my father, who coached me at basketball. I have a real competitive streak, and I am not a good loser. Sheeds knew that and kept challenging me by putting me on the good players. In the 2000 Grand Final I was on Adam Yze, in round 20 I was up against Scott Camporeale, and he also played me on Brad Johnson that year – they were all better players than me, and the more he did that the more confidence it gave me that I was in the team on merit. It was a bloody good team, but I knew I deserved to be there.

Adam Ramanauskas was one of the most courageous players Essendon ever had. While fighting a dreaded disease that affected his spinal chord, he still came back strong and kept on playing. He now has a wonderful family life and continues to work for AFL as a player manager.

There was another thing that Sheeds did that helped us become a good team – every three or four weeks or so, on a Monday, just to break things up a bit, he would take us to the local pub in Essendon, O'Sullivans, and we'd listen to stories of where he grew up, or the games he had played, and the blokes would stay there for hours just taking it all in. It wasn't about the next game or the club, it was just about getting to know each other, because it's hard to get to know the coach if he won't let his guard down.

The players appreciated that, and knew that Sheeds cared about them. He respects everyone regardless of their race, religion or background. Because of my Lithuanian background, I got a lot of questions from him about where my family came from, and he just loved to hear those stories. I was very lucky to be at the club and to have Kevin as my coach, whether it was in my first couple of years as a player, or when I was ill, which happened three times, because Kevin was always there for me.

Adam Ramanauskas, premiership player at Essendon.

OPPOSITE TOP: Micky's not smiling, a clear sign that this was during a serious head-to-head game. Amazing effort for a kid from Ballarat to go on to coach three premierships.

OPPOSITE BOTTOM: A contrast to the last photo: Mick must have been smashing me here. Mick's always had a fun side. In fact, he and Jimmy Jess became the greatest pranksters at Richmond after I left. There was certainly a lot of fun had the day someone left a baby pig in Michael Roach's locker – though I suppose it wasn't so fun for the pig. Jimmy and Mick were always finding ways to make the team laugh, but they were still ferocious on the ground.

ABOVE: In Form Three I thought 'algebra' was the capital of Algeria, and I thought it was a load of crock. But it's essential for AFL drafting. Coaches have to keep track of a rotating door of 1000-plus players every year, and they need to be able to estimate their potential value for the club minus the chance of injury and depression – which is setting in as a big consideration in recruitment. If you don't know your algebra, it will cost your club in the future.

These are three of my favourite people in footy.

ABOVE: With Denis Pagan in 2002, who I played against back at tech school. In 1998 a comment of mine comparing Kangaroos officials Greg Miller and Mark Dawson to a white and pink marshmallow (respectively) caused a bit of a stir. Roos fans turned up to throw marshmallows at us, but it turned out to be a win for both the AFL and the confectionary industry. The Marshmallow Match drew 71,154, the best crowd ever for a qualifying final, and a win for both clubs.

OPPOSITE TOP: Leigh Matthews, a magnificent player who made it into my team of the half-century, and a truly great coach.

OPPOSITE BOTTOM: Two knockabouts doing a bit of PR in Anzac week. I think Hollywood Eddie has been great for Collingwood. People should never forget the position they were in when he took on the role – broke and unsuccessful – and where he took them. Given our similar upbringing we're both very proud of our Orders of Australia. Eddie wears his everywhere.

THROUGH THE NOUGHTIES

ESSENTIALLY, 2001 SHOULD HAVE BEEN A repeat of 2000. People had been calling us the greatest Essendon team ever. As in 1985 when the local paper in Essendon predicted a hat-trick of flags in 1986, caution was required. In my view, we would only be a great side if we won more than one premiership. Thanks to Leigh Matthews, who ended up with his own hat-trick, we just missed out in 2001. Leigh has never forgiven Essendon for ending his playing career on a losing note in the 1985 Grand Final. He got us back in 1990 at Collingwood, and again as coach of Brisbane in 2001. Remember his quote that year? 'If it bleeds you can kill it.' We bled after that grand final. How you do put a band-aid on a broken heart?

We were the minor premiers on percentages, just ahead of the Lions. They were on a huge winning streak: 15 games, after beating us in Round 10. Between the start of the 1999 and the end of the 2001 season, Essendon only lost 11 games, but gee could we pick some big ones to lose – a preliminary final by one point, and a grand final. James apologised to the Essendon supporters for letting them down after that grand final, and we had.

Getting Dean Rioli to 100 games in 2006 was a highlight of the noughties for me. Dean was a beautiful kick, one of the best disposers of the ball I have ever coached. When he got the ball, our eyes would light up like Luna Park. People, and one of them might have been Kevin Bartlett, joked on radio that Dean would play in his 97th, 98th, 99th and 100th game, even if it required an ambulance and a defibrillator to get him onto the field. There were also people who said we got him to 100 games for the father–son rule. That was rubbish. When you aren't going to win a premiership, you should reward your warriors for being loyal.

James Hird is one of the best and most loyal of players in my time at Essendon – one of the four amigos: Hird, Simon Madden, Tim Watson and Gavin Wanganeen, who are hard to split. Tim Watson needed a bit of encouragement to keep going after the taggers had given him a couple of whacks, but after that he was always a superstar.

With his other three amigos – Michael Long, Dean Rioli and Derek Kickett – Gavin Wanganeen taught the rest of us that there were lots of better things to do with the football than just kick it towards the goals and hope. Simon Madden was the best tap ruckman in the history of the game and he could also kick goals. When you have the second-best tap ruckman in the game who can also kick goals, you put him up forward, which is what we did with Paul Salmon.

Meanwhile, behind the scenes, things were shifting. 🏈

2001. An ugly shot for an ugly year where we lost the grand final. At least the man behind me is having a laugh.

TIME TO LEAVE

JAMES HIRD AND I HAVE BEEN THROUGH SO MUCH together. He had the courage to come back from two major injuries, one to his foot and one that rearranged his face – though the plastic surgeon could have done something about those ears when he put it back together. Only joking, James. After the early years (particularly the 1993 Grand Final where he got ahead of himself and started celebrating before the siren so we threatened to drag him) James Hird pretty much didn't need a coach. All you had to do was make sure he got to the ground on time.

In 2007 we shared our last games at Essendon together – me as coach, him as player. It had been my idea to continue to coach on in 2008 and prepare James Hird to take over, but that all ended in July when the Essendon board chose a different approach. I didn't know that Neale Daniher, who was coach of Melbourne, would be out of a job by the end of the season. He was interviewed for the Essendon job, and I still don't get why he wasn't chosen. Since then, Neale has continued to show what a great leader he is, first with the AFL Coaches Association, which he helped turn into the highly professional outfit it is today, and now, after being diagnosed with motor neurone disease, organising the Big Freeze to help with research into finding a cure.

As for James, a succession plan seemed logical – that most uncommon of things, common sense. James would have played on in 2008, then been moved into a coaching role under a more experienced coach – me.

But others thought differently. I wonder how wise they think that decision was now?

The press conference announcing that I was leaving Essendon in 2007, which took place just after a win in Sydney. On reflection, I think it's a bad idea announcing that a coach is leaving so far ahead of time. The team gets fired up for you the following week, but then things fall away and they lose concentration as they wonder about their future.

The second-last game with Essendon for Hird and myself – and it was against my old team Richmond. A bittersweet moment.

Saying goodbye ain't easy. Essendon have had ten years of trouble since this day, and it's partly down to lack of experience in the leadership. An experienced coach who'd done a lot of interviews would never have let Dank in the club. Experience also teaches you that there are no shortcuts. My assistant coaches prove that: once they'd taken the time to gain some insights and experience, they all went on to become great, strong coaches.

The one time Sheeds got it wrong

Kevin Sheedy once wrote that he didn't think we could be friends – that we were too different. Kevin is rarely wrong, but he was on this occasion. Maybe we are different, but a desire to succeed, a love of football and a passion for the Essendon Football Club have bought us very close, and I am glad to say we are good friends.

As an Essendon supporter, I was in awe of the great Kevin Sheedy. I sat in the stands and watched three grand finals in a row from 1983 to 1985: I cried as the Bombers were outplayed in 1983, screamed with joy as Sheedy coached the Bombers to their first premiership in 19 years in 1984,

and admired the class of a champion team as they swept all before them in 1985.

As a player, I was privileged to be coached by a giant of the game; Sheeds was a great coach. In 1993, after reinventing himself, he gave a group of 18- and 19-year-old kids the confidence to take on the best in the competition. And again in 1999, he reinvented himself to produce a team that came out of nowhere to have the single most successful season in the club's history in the year 2000.

Sheeds as a coach evolved over the 27 years he was at Essendon – from a scary, dominant taskmaster to a considerate thinker who was worried as much about the game, and life as a whole, as the next match he was coaching. Kevin could still be hard in his later years. When he got fired up he was as scary as ever, but it was not the bluff or bluster that made you play better, it was his ability to make you believe you could win and succeed.

Every coach has a definitive strength. Sheeds was a good tactician, understood people and knew how to train a team, but most of all he knew how to motivate his players.

> He made us feel special, like we were playing more than a football game and that the Bombers were the good guys. That we were on the right side. Yes, Carlton and Collingwood were big clubs, but as he would say, they were the evil empire. We were lucky and we were special because we played for Essendon.

Between 1999 and 2001 we only won one premiership, but it was a special time, particularly in the year 2000, when we ran onto the field thinking we could not lose. Sheeds guided us that year, challenging us when we relaxed too much, but he knew he had a team more powerful than the others. He wound us up a few times. Carlton and North Melbourne were games with a little extra niggle. He would show videos of previous losses and read

out comments from players at those two clubs, which Sheeds knew would upset and motivate us.

He also showed he cared for his players, a side I had not seen in him before. Yes, he had always stuck up for and protected his players, but from that year on he showed a side that went beyond football. Maybe it was my age and the fact that Tania and I had our first child, but Sheeds revealed a genuine, caring nature towards many of us from that point on.

Sheeds's last two games in 2007, round 21 at the MCG against Richmond and the last round in Perth a week later, were both very special and very sad for all of us. In the end, I don't think he went out the way he should have. Hindsight is a wonderful thing, but he should have been given the chance to transition, pass the baton in a different way. He left too big a hole. Kevin Sheedy was great for the Essendon Football Club. Whatever one thought of his antics or side shows, he set the club up on a path of dominance and protected all of us. When he was in Sydney, he was sorely missed as both a coach and an important figure at the EFC. It's great that he's back.

James Hird, two-time Essendon premiership player and former club captain and coach.

OPPOSITE: Deep thought with James Hird.

With Hird and his kids Stephanie and Alex, saying a sad farewell to Essendon. Great to see my Richmond mob in background.

I always took what opportunities I could to promote the game. This rollercoaster shot was a spruik for an Essendon v Sydney game in 2001, and I was meant to be joined by Swans coach Rodney Eade but Rodney never turned up. So here I am, all alone at a theme park in western Sydney, years before I went to the Giants.

8

PROMOTING FOOTY

One of my biggest goals in footy was to be good to the game that has been so good to me. I'm motivated daily by the idea of being a positive force for football, and I cherish the friendships with the kindred spirits I've met along the way.

IGNITING DREAMS

BACK WHEN I WAS HEADED FOR RETIREMENT from Richmond and preparing for a life after playing football, Bruce Andrew, a wonderful Collingwood person (if that's not a contradiction), gave me an opportunity that helped change my life.

Bruce was on the Australian National Football Council, the national governing body for Australian Rules before the days of the AFL. He'd heard that I had been running 'pie-nights' around the Richmond area and that I was 'pretty good with the kids'. So he offered me the chance to go to Tasmania as a development officer and conduct training clinics — my first professional job in football.

I worked with legends like Darrel Baldock and Alan 'Bull' Richardson (Matthew's dad) and the reports back must have been good because I was offered a job as the VFL's first full-time development officer, going into schools to spread the message.

I was lucky to have some good teachers — the teachers themselves — who were very patient with me, helping me improve my skills in working with young people. I knew we had to move fast: the Australian soccer team under Rale Rasic had qualified for the 1974 World Cup, and Rale himself knew the value of development programs. The people running soccer at that time didn't; they sacked him, and it took 32 years for the Socceroos to get to another World Cup.

The VFL/AFL went the opposite way, employing more development officers and setting up programs like AusKick, and when you look at the game today, you'd have to say they've done a pretty good job. 🏉

OPPOSITE: *A footy clinic out at Waverley, teaching kids how to kick (on my non-preferred foot). I enjoyed the clinics enormously and have probably done about 2000 in my life. I learned just as much teaching at clinics as I did on the footy field. It probably set up my coaching career.*

ABOVE: *Giving young people direction to follow their dreams and go for it in their lives is a crucial part of what I enjoy doing. These days I also do the same for companies, giving them confidence to keep developing through their mid-years.*

LEFT: *I'll never stop chasing knowledge, or passing it on.*

A football camp at Ballarat in May 1985. What a gathering of future coaches and managers of AFL. This is one of the most amazing photos I have. Developing kids into players is only part of it: it's also important to look after the coaches and managers of the future. Here we were getting promising players in to build their skills and confidence in coaching, development and media, and the list of young coaches-to-be who attended speaks for itself.

Coaches: Barry Mitchell (Swans), Danny Frawley (St Kilda), Chris Connolly (Melbourne), Peter Curran (Hawthorn), Richard Osbourne (Fitzroy), Gary Pert (Fitzroy), Robert Flower (Melbourne), Kevin Sheedy (Coaching Director and Essendon Coach), Geoff Miles (Director Australian Sports Camp), Shane Ward (Melbourne), Gerard Healy (Melbourne), Mark Thompson (Essendon), Shane Heard (Essendon).

Coaches' assistants: Allistair Clarkson, Brad Haskett, Michael Troon, Michael Devlin, Michael McGuane, Craig Hosking, Craig Pertzel, David Morris.

BUILDING BLOCKBUSTERS

I'VE BEEN LUCKY TO BE INVOLVED IN FOOTBALL AT A time of huge growth for the sport, right back from my first years as Essendon coach in the 1980s. With two flags to celebrate, the Essendon board members who hadn't been too happy with me after the 1983 Grand Final dinner were off my back by 1985, and I had the opportunity to look at the bigger picture – the future of the club, and indeed the game.

The world of sport was changing rapidly back then. Tennis had gone professional; Essendon supporter Greg Chappell, and Dennis Lillee and Rod Marsh had led Australia's cricketers through a revolution with World Series Cricket, and Australian Rules football had to make sure it wasn't left behind. I was determined to leave Essendon better off than when I'd arrived, and the same went for the code in general. I argued that if we wanted to have more full-time people like assistant coaches and a full-time recruiting person in Noel Judkins, we had to market ourselves better to generate the necessary revenue. I showed the marketing man at Essendon all the empty places at Windy Hill where he could put sponsor signs, and he probably didn't like me much after that.

As we got better at our marketing and bringing in more members, we had to think about leaving Windy Hill for the MCG. It caused a lot of division, but time shows it was a good decision. When you look at the crowds Essendon gets at the MCG, not just for blockbusters but for most of its home and away games, well, how could we ever have fitted them all in at Windy Hill (even if we could have convinced the bowls club to move)?

With so much else for people to choose from, we had to ensure that footy was competing in the entertainment stakes and give people reason to attend. The best reason is winning, but you don't get to do that all the time. So we came up with ideas like the Anzac Day match to say thanks to the serving men and women of Australia. We had to work long and hard to get that one up and running, but well done Gubby Allan for coming on board when he was at Collingwood. The first Anzac Day clash was in 1995.

And thank you, Richmond, for agreeing to Dreamtime at the 'G, first played in 2005 though it already feels like an older tradition. There could only be two clubs involved in that game: Richmond and Essendon. Black, red and yellow, the colours of the Aboriginal flag.

And keeping up the record of inventing one new blockbuster game every decade, I'm delighted that Essendon is part of the Country Game between Essendon and Geelong, letting the regional people of Australia know they haven't been forgotten. ●

ABOVE: Mal Michaels, a wonderful player whose grandfather Ume Kone was a 'Fuzzy Wuzzy Angel', one of the incredible Papua New Guinean people who served as transporters on the Kokoda Track, carrying supplies, ammunition and wounded Australian soldiers. How brilliant that decades on, a man whose grandfather gave so much to Australians could become a champion of Aussie Rules and do so much to bring it to the young people of Papua New Guinea.

LEFT: Great to promote the Country Game with Tom Hawkins and Joe Daniher, a new face from a great footballing family.

Spreading the message as far as it'll go: since the first Anzac Day match in 1995, around 2 million people have come through the turnstiles for this special event.

Mick Malthouse and myself standing with Bruce Ruxton, President of the RSL for over 20 years and the man who said yes to the Anzac Day match. The first official Anzac Day clash in 1995 drew a full house at the MCG, with another 20,000 people left outside, who gathered in the Fitzroy Gardens and listened to the game on the radio.

Sheeds the 'feminist'

It doesn't seem right to describe Kevin Sheedy as a feminist, but he definitely promotes equal rights regardless of gender, and was well ahead of his time recognising women in football.

In recent years we have celebrated many 'firsts' for women: the AFL women's season, the first female umpire to adjudicate at League level and, finally, a woman in the mix on *The Footy Show*. While in isolation these are all 'firsts', they are inextricably linked to the ground work of all the women who have gone before; this is something that Kevin was keen to acknowledge nearly 20 years ago.

Around the centenary year of the AFL, Kevin realised that there was not any official acknowledgement of women in football, so he decided he would write a book himself: *Football's Women – the Forgotten Heroes*. He wanted to listen to, understand and amplify the voices of 'the other team', the women who, in Kevin's formative years, inspired, encouraged and coached him in football; but even more, it was the women around the club that respected and nurtured him on a personal level.

We met to discuss the format of the book, and to determine which women he wanted to include. I don't know why I was surprised to find that his office was packed floor to ceiling with books; he is an avid reader and deep thinker. He was also studying Emmeline Pankhurst, the leader of the suffragette movement in Britain and, ironically, it was him that inspired me to do the same.

For the book, Kevin wanted to highlight the contributions of those women who were mentors in his life: his mother with her incredible work ethic; his wife, Geraldine, who he says almost singlehandedly brought up their four children; his family, with their unconditional support; his first teacher at St Joseph's Primary, Sister Rupert; his first coach, teenager Veronica Nolan, who ignited his passion for footy; and the women at Prahran Football Club – Mrs Seedy, Mrs Pearson and Mrs Simmons – who had treated him with the utmost respect and care, and who had helped shape his outlook.

He wanted to acknowledge the women behind *all* the players and the coaches, and those women throughout every level of the game.

Over too many cappuccinos, and many meetings in cafes and Kevin's 'mobile office' at the Botanic Gardens, the list of women grew and grew. Every person who contributed had their own story, and each was fascinating. I was so lucky and privileged to be a part of the process. The journey for me in writing the book with Kevin was probably just like another of his coaching endeavours; he set the parameters and the goals, provided the coaching and then let me attempt to achieve my best performance. With his insight and input, together we could produce a wonderful snapshot of the role of women in football.

It was fantastic to meet Tess Stynes (mother of Jim Stynes, Melbourne) in the iconic Bewley's coffee shop in Dublin. Kevin particularly wanted Indigenous Australians to contribute their stories, which took me to the Top End to meet Michael Long and his brother Steven, to capture their memories of their mother. I went to Far North Queensland to speak with June McLean (mother of Michael McLean, Footscray, Brisbane) and to Darwin to speak with Barbara Chisolm (mother of Scott Chisolm, Fremantle, Melbourne). In Melbourne, former Premier Joan Kirner spoke to us in her Spring St office and articulated her 'one red eye, one black eye' devotion to Essendon developed on the boundary at Windy Hill.

There was a meeting with Caro Wilson (Chief Football Writer, *The Age*) about how she had forged her career in football journalism and more coffee at Rhumbaralla's Cafe in Brunswick St, Fitzroy, where I spoke to Lisa Hardeman, a player, coach and honorary president of the Victorian Women's Football League. I met Irene Chatfield, the fanatical Footscray supporter who famously helped save the club from a merger with Fitzroy in 1989, which seems incredible given the Bulldogs finally became premiers in 2016. Even my own mother, Joyce Brown, had some insights about her experiences as the 'Coach from left field' on ABC radio with Tim Lane before each AFL match.

It is timely to reflect on how far women have come in the past 20 years. Ahead of its time, our book was a testament to the way Kevin Sheedy views life and acknowledges how women have helped shape his opportunities and who he is to this very day.

Carolyn Brown, co-author of **Football's Women: The Forgotten Heroes.**

ABOVE: Geraldine looks like she's got a better hold of the 2000 premiership cup than I do. Women have long been a major contributor to our game, often in silence, and Geraldine is a perfect example. My wife has known me for six of the premierships I've been involved in, raising our four kids while I was playing and then coaching. But she rarely spoke out about it. In Geraldine's first and last media 'interview', she opened the front door to find the journalists, said 'It's not easy living with Kevin,' and closed the door again. The next day it was front page of the Herald Sun. She swore she'd never speak to them again.

OPPOSITE: My superstar mother was always one of my greatest ever influences, and her smile shows just how happy she'd been in her life. Heading to 80 and still smiling – what a great energy to pass on.

PROMOTING FOOTY FROM WITHIN

RIGHT FROM THE START OF MY FOOTBALL career there had always been big hopes about spreading Aussie Rules internationally. But for me, our first responsibility was to spread it to every part of Australia, and particularly to our underrepresented Indigenous communities.

Michael Long and Nicky Winmar changed Australian football forever; through their deeds and daring they turned on the tap and Aboriginal men flooded into the game, making it even more electrifying and truly Australian. Winmar did it that day at Victoria Park in 1993 when he lifted his shirt, pointed to his skin and shouted to the Collingwood cheer squad, 'I'm black and I am proud to be black!' Longie did it off and on the field – he's the Pelé of Australian rules. He taught me so much about football and about my country. He learned a bit of history from me too. He didn't know that a lot of people who came out to Australia from 1778 weren't keen on the idea, particularly the Irish convicts. When he discovered the Sheedys were Irish rather than English, I think it helped us get on.

The most important thing Michael – along with Gavin Wanganeen, Derek Kickett and Dean Rioli – taught me was vision on the football field. Before those three came to Essendon a lot of the time our players would look up, bomb the ball towards the goal and hope for a contest. They would look around, find spaces that nobody else could see and kick the ball there. Asking them how they did it would be a bit like asking Elvis how he sang and swivelled his hips at the same time: you don't, you just sit back and enjoy the song lines.

Nicky Winmar's second name is Elvis, which probably explains why he was such a good player. Football has gained a lot from this brand-new recruiting zone, which stretches from the Tiwi Islands, to the home of the Noongar people in Western Australia, to Gavin Wanganeen's forebears near Ceduna in South Australia. Once they began to feel welcome, Aboriginal footballers brought so much to our game. Between Joe Johnson in 1904 and the end of the 1970s only a handful of Aboriginal people played in the VFL. In the 1980s there were 29 including Longie, who made his debut in 1989. In the 2017 season there are more than 80 – men and women. That I played any part in making that happen is one of my proudest achievements during 50 years in footy. 🏉

ABOVE: Michael Long, a boy from the Tiwi Islands, and James Hird, a boy from Canberra, standing together on Anzac Day. That to me is a classic shot of Australia. Bringing people in our country together was one of the best things we did at Essendon, extending our reach beyond our old zone. It's important to remember that Michael Long was only the 30th Indigenous player to play in the VFL/AFL. In all that time, how did that happen?!

LEFT: Congratulating the late Maurice Rioli at an Aboriginal Team of the Century event. Great to be at their night. Beside him is Gavin Wanganeen from Port Lincoln, and behind them are Mickey O'Loughlin and Byron Pickett. Maurice was one of the early great players in the VFL who went to Richmond. The number of brilliant footballers who've come from the Tiwi Islands, with its population of 4000, is quite amazing.

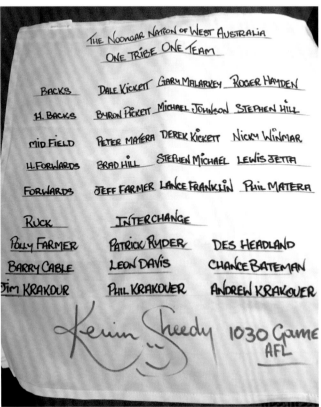

The Noongar Nation of West Australia
One Tribe One Team

BACKS	Dale Kickett	Gary Malarkey	Roger Hayden
H. BACKS	Byron Pickett	Michael Johnson	Stephen Hill
MID FIELD	Peter Matera	Derek Kickett	Nicky Winmar
H. FORWARDS	Brad Hill	Stephen Michael	Lewis Jetta
FORWARDS	Jeff Farmer	Lance Franklin	Phil Matera

RUCK INTERCHANGE
Polly Farmer   Patrick Ryder   Des Headland
Barry Cable   Leon Davis   Chance Bateman
Jim Krakour   Phil Krakouer   Andrew Krakouer

Kevin Sheedy 1030 Game AFL

TOP LEFT: *A young fella from up north presenting me with a fishing spear. The artwork behind us featuring Michael Long is a classic piece of Essendon Football Club at Windy Hill, created by the Essendon board to show the history of the club and commemorate players of the past.*

TOP RIGHT: *Doesn't hurt to say hello to a race of people who have been on the continent for 65,000 years. We finally got it right at AFL clubs. In the past, Victorian clubs were more blind than most – the VFL only had 28 Indigenous players in over a hundred years of existence; slightly pathetic, I would think. There've been 330 signed since.*

BOTTOM LEFT: *While on a flight one day I decided to jot down my personal best Noongar Nation team – mostly AFL/VFL players, so WA is underrepresented here. Of course, it's not linked to the real Indigenous Team of the Century, which was selected by Indigenous leaders and elders – just the thoughts of an Irish man flying over the Nullarbor and appreciating what an amazing group of players our Indigenous communities have produced.*

BOTTOM RIGHT: *I'd been told more than once that the Indigenous boys on the team wouldn't like mud. What a load of bulldust. Do you think I'm an Irishman with no brains?*

He always came back for me

My career should have ended at 96 games. My knees were gone. I would have operations to remove bone spurs to give me more flexibility, and then I would start to run again and more bits of bone would drop off. Eventually after four operations the Essendon club doctor, Bruce Reid, told me that was it. He mustn't have told Kevin, because in 2006 he did everything he could to get me to 100 games.

It might have been because of the father–son rule, or it might be because when I first arrived at Essendon for the 1998 season, we had a conversation in which Kevin asked me what my goals were, and I told him I would love to get to 100 games and get my name on my locker.

Thanks to Kevin, I played my 100th, and last, game on 26 August 2006. If the knees hadn't already sent me a message that it was time to give up, a broken wrist in that game certainly did.

That meeting when I talked about wanting to play 100 games wasn't the first one with Kevin. That had happened when I was playing in the WAFL with South Fremantle. We had played on the Saturday at Subiaco. Essendon were due to play there the next day, and the Bombers came out to have a practice run after our game had finished.

When I left Subi, my car broke down just outside the ground and, without a mobile phone back then, I wasn't sure how I was going to get home. Then the Essendon bus came along, and out came Kevin Sheedy to see if he could help. He waved the bus to go on, and he sat and waited with me until John Todd, the South Fremantle coach, gave us both a lift.

I introduced myself to Kevin when he got out of the bus, but I have no idea if he knew who I was back then. As far as I was concerned I was just another Indigenous boy on the side of the road with a broken-down car, but this became the symbol of Kevin to me. He always came back for me.

Whenever I fell back at Essendon he would come back for me and get me up to the level of playing AFL again. This is something I still find hard to talk about now, 15 years later, but when I was at Essendon, I suffered from depression. Only four people at the club knew – Robert Shaw, John Quinn, Bruce Reid and Kevin. When I was in this dark place and would say to Kevin that football was my job and that I was letting everyone down because I couldn't play he would say, 'Oi, it's not about the football, it's about getting you right.'

It was a huge thrill for me to be picked up by Essendon. I always loved the Bombers – on my bedroom wall I had pictures of Kevin, Michael Long, all the Bombers. I will never forget my first game, coming off the rookie list. It was Michael Long's first game as captain, and Matthew Lloyd kicked 13 goals. Coming from the Tiwi Islands I've known since early on that Kevin is something special. He is God to all the people living in remote Australia. He always brought Essendon to play in the Northern Territory, but the Tiwi Islanders hold him in even higher regard than that because he gave us a go. He was pretty much the front-runner in giving Indigenous boys the chance to play in the AFL.

Even though I have been retired for more than a decade, Kevin still comes back for me, just not on a footy field. Because of my own mental health issues, and because I am aware that it is a real problem in the Northern Territory, I set up the Rioli Fund to help the Menzies School of Health Research, which is doing a lot of good work in Indigenous communities. We'd be working on the accounts and these amounts would turn up that we didn't know anything about, so we'd have to go back to the people who paid them into the fund and ask them for more details. They would tell us that Kevin Sheedy had done a speaking engagement – it might be in Tasmania, it might be in Perth – and that he had asked them to put his speaker's fee into the Rioli Foundation. There'd be amounts like $5000, a lot of money, and he wouldn't tell us he had done it.

I missed the 2000 Grand Final because I was injured in the only game we lost that year, against the Bulldogs. I was probably injured a lot more than I was fit during my career, but I got to 100 games, I got my name on a locker at Essendon. That would never have happened if not for one person.

Dean Rioli, who played 100 games for Essendon.

Dean Rioli was a wonderful, powerhouse player. A knee injury nearly robbed him of his career goal to make 100 games.

Passion and fire

'**Don't come back with a leg missing!**' That was how Kevin would farewell me whenever I was going home to South Australia, where I would go spear-fishing off the Eyre Peninsula and swimming among the sharks. Amazingly, he could talk to me about my fishing trips with my family, and knew how much I loved them, from the day I walked in the door to Essendon as a 17-year-old. I realised that's the way Kevin is; he takes the time to find out everything about his players, their family, their hobbies, how they're feeling, not just how well they might play footy for him.

My love for my family and the lifestyle in South Australia brought about one of the toughest conversations in my life, talking to Kevin about the possibility of going home when Port Adelaide came into the AFL in 1997. I had butterflies in my stomach whenever the topic came up. It was very much a flip of the coin at the end. There was a discussion where Sheeds was trying to encourage me to stay and hoping I would, but eventually I decided to leave. I loved Essendon and I love Sheeds, and he's been a great supporter of mine, so for him to still have that respect there after I left, that is very important to me. It means a lot to me – people who I respect, what they think and how they treat me.

There was a time in 2000 when Essendon won another flag and I thought I might have made the wrong decision. It was something that burned in my gut for a long time and I said to myself then that if I didn't play in another winning grand final before I retired, it would have been the wrong decision. Your career is all about winning premierships, and luckily enough fate went my way and Port Adelaide won in 2004.

Footy-wise, what an unbelievable motivator Kevin was – the passion and the fire in the belly that flowed through into his players ... you just wanted to play for him. He was tough when he needed to be, he expected you to play hard footy – if the ball was there and someone was in the way, you knew what you had to do.

We won a flag in 1993, but we nearly didn't because we were down by seven goals at half-time in the preliminary final. I was only young and I don't remember everything he said at half-time, but one thing that sticks in my mind was him telling the players that 'your families are out there watching you' and that we were still in the match, that we had to believe we could win it, and we had to go out there and do it for our families.

My family wasn't there that night, but whenever I cross the white line, I am playing for my family. It has always been a massive thing for me. I am representing my clan, and my people. I am from the Kokatha clan in western South Australia. Sheeds always loved his Indigenous boys: me, Michael Long, Derek Kickett, Che Cockatoo-Collins and Dean Rioli. He'd always make these little comments like 'I love the way you do that', referring to our flair and creativity, which he recognised is what you need to win premierships. People often wonder what it is that gives the Indigenous players that extra flair. Maybe it flows through our DNA after thousands of years of running through the bush chasing kangaroos.

There was certainly a lot flair involved in us jagging that premiership in 1993 when no one expected us to. In the week leading up to the grand final I had been awarded the

Brownlow Medal, the first Indigenous player win – that's precious to me. Winning the Brownlow can disrupt your preparation for a grand final, and I remember Kevin coming up to me a couple of times and saying, 'just enjoy it'. I was pleased to be able to play my role in the grand final.

Thanks to my wife, Pippa, I have a new career as an Indigenous artist. She found a painting called 'Camping at Point Pearce' that I had started back in 2003 then left un-finished, and she encouraged me to finish it.

I have family ties to the community at Point Pearce and I have plenty of memories of camping there as a kid. So I got off the couch and completed it and now have many other works. Kevin has been out there promoting for me. He's a handy marketing person to have on your side. He's the best-connected person in Australia.

Gavin Wanganeen, Brownlow Medallist and premiership player at Essendon and Port Adelaide.

A detail from 'Shooting Star' by Gavin Wanganeen, a man of many talents. Nothing better than seeing our Indigenous players proud of their heritage and embracing their culture. It's what Indigenous footy is all about.

INTERNATIONAL RULES

AFTER BEING PART OF THE GALAHS TOUR OF IRELAND in 1978 – when I even managed to visit some distant relatives – I was disappointed that by 2005 AFL officials were referring to the International Rules series as a debacle. At a meeting, I argued that the mess was all the AFL's fault because they kept appointing people to coach Australia who had never coached. The AFL conceded the point and asked Mick Malthouse to be Australia's coach, but apparently Collingwood wouldn't release him. Eventually, after getting the right assurances from chairman Ron Evans that

the AFL was fair dinkum, and after getting approval from Essendon, I agreed to do the job.

We put together a terrific team of support staff including Robert DiPierdomenico, Stephen Silvagni and Gerard Healy, as well as many with their own Irish backgrounds such as Danny Frawley, Kevin Sheehan, Jim Stynes and his brother Brian, our forward scout.

We needed to find out as much as possible about the Irish players, and we changed the selection process to pick players suited to the hybrid rules as opposed to fielding a team of All-Australians. In the first game

Near the end of my career I really enjoyed coaching players from other clubs. Selecting six Indigenous boys to compete against Ireland was really important: it gave them the chance to play for Australia, and they were deciding factors in us winning the series. Jim Stynes told me Irish people didn't know much about Aboriginal people, and I thought that was a good enough reason to play them – if they don't know the enemy they can't prepare to face them.

in Perth in 2005, we produced our highest ever score against the Irish. We also won the second game, and probably the fight. Chris Johnson, along with his teammates, had taken umbrage at the Irish players' practice of raking their opponents' shins with their sprigs. Johnson was suspended for his retaliation, an elbow that found its target, but by now the Irish knew that, from the chairman to the goalkeeper, these Galahs were a different flock.

In Ireland in 2006, that fair dinkum approach was on show when, after losing the first game by eight points, we sold out Croke Park and beat the Irish 69–31 to claim the series on aggregate. But once again there was controversy after a legitimate Danyle Pearce tackle knocked out local hero Graham Geraghty.

Seán Boylan, the Irish coach, was furious, saying: 'As far as I'm concerned what happened out there in that quarter today is

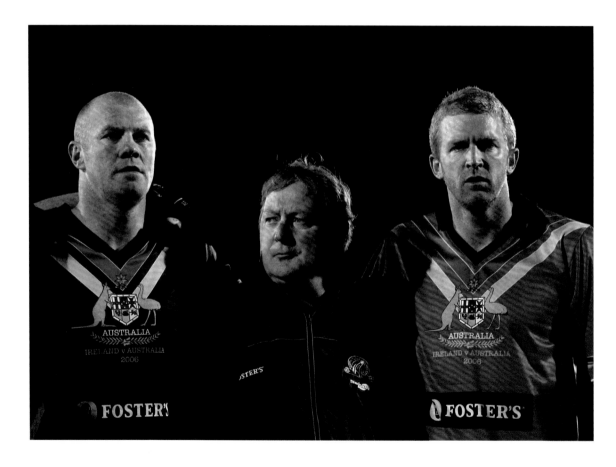

Our next two captains in Ireland after Andrew McLeod were Barry Hall in Galway and Dustin Fletcher in Dublin. When I rang Dustin to tell him he'd be captain he was on holidays in Scotland, so it would have made sense for him to just meet us in Ireland. But he flew home to Melbourne and then straight back to Ireland with the team, and I thought that was real leadership flying under the radar. When Dustin talked people listened. He had played 400 games by the time he was 40, and was the greatest Australian goalie ever.

not acceptable in any code of sport. It's not accepted on the street. How that could be termed as playing within the spirit of the game is beyond me.'

I disagreed, saying that we won the game fairly and because we were fitter. It has become a thing with the Irish that whenever we beat them, they get upset and threaten never to play Australia again. After Croke Park, there were a lot of crisis meetings and the 2007 series was called off, but they were back in 2008. And we must keep on playing each other. There has always been a strong bond between Australia and Ireland, and Irish settlers helped us develop our game. Harry Beitzel started something special in the history of sport with those Galahs tours – two countries coming together to create a new set of rules and skills to compete against each other. And with Australia trailing Ireland 10–9 in series wins, we need every opportunity to fix up that little statistic. ●

Andrew McLeod, who won the Jim Stynes Medal in Perth, was the first Indigenous captain to represent Australia against Ireland. Like Johnson, Fletcher and Hall, McLeod was never captain of his AFL team, but he was captain of the nation. It was Harry Beitzel's dream come true, and a fantastic moment for footy.

OPPOSITE TOP: *With Mary McAleese, who was president of Ireland from 1997 to 2011.*

OPPOSITE BOTTOM: *Barry Hall was one of two captains on this tour. It was important to share leadership, so more than one person got a chance to represent their country. We had Alex McLeod in Perth, Chris Johnson in Melbourne, Dustin Fletcher in Galway and Barry Hall captaining the winning match at Croke Park in Ireland.*

ABOVE: *One of the most fun times in my life was coaching Australia in International Rules. I hadn't been allowed to coach Victoria from the mid-80s onward due to my contract at Essendon, so in 2005 when the AFL asked me to coach and reinvigorate the International Rules series I was happy to be involved. We went on to win the series with over 200,000 people attending.*

The priest and the plumber

HARRY BEITZEL GENEROUSLY CONTRIBUTED TO THIS BOOK NOT LONG BEFORE HE PASSED AWAY IN August 2017. Many of us owe him a debt of gratitude, as he was the first person to offer any type of media training for players and coaches. He took groups of us to football and netball functions, where he taught us how to use a microphone and present ourselves in a professional manner. He taught us how to deliver enthusiastic presentations that would help young people to develop a positive approach to life and their chosen sports.

In addition to myself, some others who were trained by Harry include Kevin Bartlett, Sam Newman, Joyce Brown and Eddie McGuire.

We all salute you, Harry, and thank you.

Kevin Sheedy is a winner because he knows how to learn from a loss. I first said that about him years ago, and nothing has changed. He learns from everything: losses, books, talking to people in the street. He never misses an opportunity to gain more knowledge.

He reckons I didn't like him early on in our relationship because, as an umpire, I didn't like players who broke the rules – and he might have been right. But over time, as I got to know him better, that changed.

I first met Kevin when Tom Hafey asked me to speak to his players before the 1967 Grand Final, a motivational talk I called 'Up on Cloud 9', which was all about living out your dreams. Kevin says hearing that presentation changed his life. He missed the 1967 Grand Final because of injury, but he made a pledge to himself to live out his dream of playing in a grand final.

By the time Tom Hafey asked me to address the team again before the 1969 grand final, Kevin had grown into the player that everyone at Richmond loved – if not people at other clubs. He was tough and, when asked to be, he was ruthless. The opposition's best players always kept one eye on the ball and one eye on Kevin Sheedy.

But there was another side to Kevin that was also emerging. Kevin's passion for developing the game was there even then, as a regular member of the Cadbury coaching clinics in the country. That's where I really got to know him.

As well as Cloud 9, he wanted to know all about the media, public relations and marketing. I had my own PR company, and was also calling the football on radio. The knowledge I could give Kevin was different to what he was being taught at Richmond by Tom Hafey and Graeme Richmond, who were mainly focused on doing what was best for the Tigers.

He was always asking me questions. If as part of the answer to those questions I suggested he read a book, he would go away and do that and then come back and ask even more questions. In 1978, I selected him for the Galahs' tour of Ireland, and even though he broke his ankle in the first game, we had a great trip together.

And he had a great trip on his own meeting his distant kin in Ireland. Because his leg was in plaster, he couldn't drive, so Father John Brosnan, the Pentridge Prison chaplain who was with us on the tour, offered to do so. The conversation between the priest and the plumber was something to behold, I am told. Kevin – as he always does – was asking lots of questions, on this occasion about the deeper meanings of being a Catholic.

Kevin has been a loyal friend to me over many years now. He has helped me through some difficult times. He remains a man of great creativity, always searching for ideas, not just to promote football, but to help people. He does a lot of charitable things that people might not get to hear about.

Of course, he is not perfect. He always seems to be running late. That's in part because of his insatiable urge to gain more knowledge. If he meets somebody in the street and they have something interesting to say, well, the meeting he's on his way to will have to wait.

And he will tell you: 'If you want a job done, get a busy person.' Kevin Sheedy's no longer coaching, but he's still busy – and he's still late, but he's still learning.

Kevin often talks about 'thanks' being one of the most important words in the world. I'd like to say thanks to Kevin for everything that he has done for me, for football, and for Australia.

The late Harry Beitzel, former umpire, broadcaster and Hall of Fame member.

A rare sighting of Greater Western Sydney's early colours – the colours of Footscray, another great team of 'the west'. Sydney's sunsets inspired our final choice of orange as the predominate colour of the Giants.

9

THE GIANTS

From little things and all that. The Giants were built from
nothing – the grounds, the players, the whole lot – but it
was a challenge I just loved being a part of and I've no doubt
premierships will be built on that foundation.

THE MARCH INTO SYDNEY

THE NOUGHTIES WERE A TIME OF ONGOING growth for Australian Rules, to the extent that the AFL felt confident to create two new teams: the Suns and the Giants.

The crowds for AFL games in Victoria are amazing. Essendon averages 75,000 at the 'G for Anzac Day, Dreamtime, the Country Game and Round One against Hawthorn. That's for games between three suburbs of Melbourne and a regional Victorian city. If they get 15,000 to a game of Rugby League in Sydney they're happy. Why wouldn't we try and replicate that beyond the state?

In the 1980s a lot of people were against that, even the Victorian Government. When you think of all the money that comes into Victoria these days as supporters travel from Queensland, New South Wales, South Australia and Western Australia to watch their teams, it's hard to understand how anyone, let alone a state premier and treasurer, could have been so short-sighted.

Thankfully we had people like the former head of the VFL Allen Aylett who were prepared to stand up to the Government – and even endure death threats – to make our game the national winter one. Ron Barassi was prepared to put his great win–loss ratio at risk to save the Swans. When Sydney was struggling to win a game in the 1990s and the Bears were losing by a record margin to Geelong, it would have been hard to believe that in 2017 we have rivalry round in every state except Tasmania (though it's a year-round rivalry round between North and South down there).

Australian Rules football had been on a long slow march into Sydney for more than 100 years, from the first recorded game in 1877 between Carlton and Waratah, to the arrival of the Swans in 1981, which speeded things up a bit. Then, around 2008, the AFL decided it was time for a real 'quick march' and to put a team into western Sydney.

At that time I was roving ambassador for the AFL, but people started talking to me about the idea of coaching this team. After Essendon sacked me there was always this itch too sensitive to scratch about whether I would have an opportunity to coach again. Melbourne had interviewed me for their coaching job, but I suspected that the people on the panel weren't really the people running the club.

There was a different feel about the Giants. They say sport and politics should always be kept separate, but sometimes when politicians and sports people get together, good things happen, like in the 2009 Swans–Essendon game when the then-Premier of New South Wales, Nathan Rees, began talking to me about coaching Greater Western Sydney. For him, it wasn't so much about the football; it was about giving opportunities to the people of western Sydney. He thought Australian Rules had a role to play, and that appealed to me.

So after the disappointment of leaving Essendon, and knowing that people at the AFL like Andrew Demetriou were 100 per cent behind the Giants, I decided again to put all my energy into one team. It was going to be a challenge but I don't mind one of those, and the more people wailed and moaned in Sydney (hello Richard Colless) and in Melbourne (hello Eddie McGuire and the tumble weeders) the more I thought how much fun it would be to prove them wrong.

A big first day introducing the Giants to Australia. Only one of the players in this line-up is still a Giant: Jeremy Cameron.

STARTING FROM SCRATCH

SO THAT'S HOW WE WENT ABOUT IT. IT DIDN'T matter that we were pretty much a team of Year 12 students, or that we were training in parks using old tyres and anything else we could beg, borrow or steal. We were going to make it a fun experience. And how hard was it to have fun at Breakfast Point on the banks of the Parramatta River, which was like a resort? While Eddie McGuire was conjuring a 'land of falafels', in reality we were (in between some serious training) lounging around in pools, sitting on our balconies sipping coffee and, on New Year's Eve, drinking champagne and watching the fireworks over the Sydney Harbour Bridge.

Just as it is possible to love two footy clubs, it is possible to love two cities. Frank Sinatra sang about New York and Chicago. A lot of people like to sneeringly compare the Sydney and Melbourne lifestyle. Why waste your time doing that when they are both great? And one great part of Sydney, its western suburbs, was going to have a footy team called the Greater Western Sydney Giants. If you've ever watched a sunset in the Grose Valley behind Sydney, you will know why we chose orange as the team's predominate colour: the sandstone glows orange as the sun dips behind the Blue Mountains. And further west, behind those Blue Mountains,

OPPOSITE: Planning a list for the Giants' future.

TOP: Decision-making in the hallways of Rooty Hill RSL while the Giants' home is still under construction. You've got to take your first step somewhere in life, but you never know where you will end up.

BOTTOM: Roughing it. A bin and some ice works just as well as anything you'll find in a state-of-the-art sports facility. Some great players in the making here include Andrew Phillips (first bin on the left) who is now with Carlton, Josh Bruce (first bin on the right) who is now with St Kilda and Nathan Wilson (standing with the towel) still with the Giants.

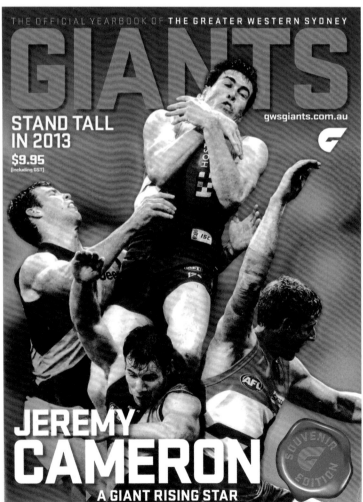

ABOVE: History tells you not many full-forwards become great coaches, but John Longmire has bucked the trend and become an amazing one. As a player he kicked 500-plus goals – not easy when you're always the second option because Wayne Carey is on your team. He played in a premiership in his last game, coached a premiership in his second year and has been a good ally promoting the game in Sydney.

LEFT: Promoting the Giants.

is a town called Orange. We couldn't wait to get there, and what a welcome we got from the local schoolkids when we did – although it was hard to tell our players and the schoolkids apart.

We had two fine young co-captains in Phil Davis and Callan Ward, and a wonderful young man from Rugby League, Israel Folau, who was very much the gentle Giant off the field. His decision to leave Rugby League had angered a lot of people in that game; his decision to go to Rugby Union when he decided that Australian Rules Football was not quite his game angered them even further. One columnist kept spelling his name I$rael, implying he was money-hungry. I have been involved in senior sport for more than 50 years and rate Israel as one of the most honest and genuine people I know. When he looked me in the eye and told me he was leaving, I could only say 'thank you'. He had helped open so many doors for us in Sydney's west.

Israel also played his part in a wonderful day at Canberra's Manuka Oval in 2012, our inaugural season, when we beat the Suns for our first precious four pints. Oh what a feeling to sing the song for the *first* time after winning an AFL game! I can still see the glint in Israel's eye that day, because he knew he had made a big contribution. I'd like to think that we in turn contributed to that brilliant aerial try he scored for the Wallabies against Scotland in June 2017. Is it possible that the mark of the year might just have been taken in a Rugby Union Test?!?

I also clearly remember the stony faces and silence of 17,000 people at Kardinia Park in June of that first season when the score was 45 points each at half-time. We had come up with a game plan that matched the Cats. Their more experienced players took the game away from us in the second half, but it was an early sign that when these GWS boys became men, they were going to be special.

The arrival of Israel, followed by a lot of talented players via draft concessions, didn't go down well with people in Melbourne, who were still hanging on to the idea that Australian Rules Football was Victoria's game. To me it was common sense to give the Giants and the Suns every chance to succeed. My last game as coach was against the Suns on their home ground. It was an almost perfect Queensland winter's day – except we lost. As the sun set on my coaching journey, I couldn't help but marvel: my first senior game as a coach had been for a Melbourne suburb; my last was for the west of Sydney, and played on a ground in south-east Queensland. The game had come a long way.

It won't be long before the Giants win a flag (if they haven't already by the time this book is printed). From training in parks, the Giants now have purpose-built training facilities and a new home ground. In 2017, they still have Phil Davis and Callan Ward, two of the most experienced leaders in the game. If you build the foundations properly, the home will never fall. But for me, another home was calling: Essendon. ⬤

Sheedy the psychologist

I didn't want the captaincy of the Giants when Kevin first offered it to me. I hadn't told him I didn't want it, but I had told Graeme Allan, the football manager, and maybe Choco Williams, one of the assistant coaches, saying I didn't think I was ready for it and wanted to concentrate on my own game. One day Kevin said he wanted to have a chat with me and while driving me to training said he wanted me to be captain.

Kevin said it would be the best thing for me as a footballer and a person to be captain, and wondered why I wouldn't want to go for it. And with that, my mind was changed. That was as co-captain with Luke Power and Phil Davis, who like me was only 21. But we were experienced compared to the rest of the 18-year-olds at the club at the time.

That chat established a special bond between me and Sheeds. It wasn't like that when I first met him, though, because I was bit intimidated. I grew up barracking for Essendon and he was a legend of the game in my eyes and was one of my father's favourite people.

You hear all the stories about how, back in the day, he was ruthless. But he was very nurturing of the players at the Giants, and a great influence on all of us. Sometimes you might laugh at the way he got his message across. One time he had us all watching a video of the last game we had played and he was trying to teach us about ball movement and inside-50 kicks. He paused the vision at a time when the opposition had filled all the holes and then started talking to us about hitting a target, saying, 'Look at this gap here, you've got to be good enough to hit this on your left foot, on your right foot, under pressure and when you're not under pressure.' We all looked at each other because the kick was near impossible – if you pulled it off it would be the best you'd ever seen in your life, but I guess he was giving us the message that if you want to play in the AFL, you must have that level of skill. There was always a lot of psychological stuff when you were talking with Sheeds, whether it was just you, or whether he was talking to the whole team.

When we won our first game against the Gold Coast down in Canberra we were all happy, but he seemed to be more joyous than any of us, dancing around when we sang the team song. It probably meant even more to him than it did to us, because of what he was doing in Sydney. Day to day, we'd spend more time with Choco Williams, when Sheeds would be doing a lot of work expanding the game, raising money for the training centre and stadium, and being a Giants salesman, but he was head coach on game day.

One of the great ideas Kevin had was to have us all living in the one suburb, Breakfast Point on the Parramatta River. I was there for one year, and the club still encourages the young players to live there 24/7. You get the meals from the restaurant and we had swimming pools, gymnasium facilities, and the bond we built was massive.

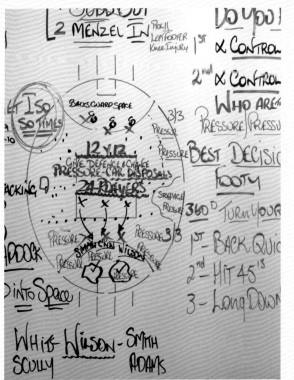

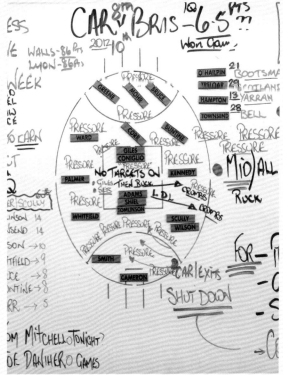

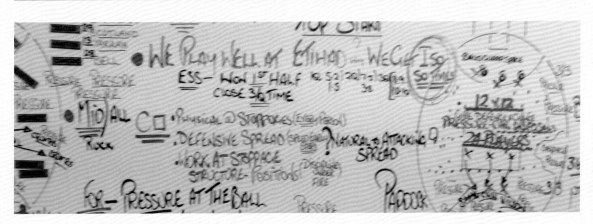

I didn't quite have the view of the river and the Sydney Harbour Bridge that Sheeds had from the balcony of his apartment – if you had dogs you had to live in the ground-floor townhouses – so I missed the fireworks on New Year's Eve. Though I am sure if I'd asked, he would have invited me around. He's always been a good man to me, and I owe him a lot.

Callan Ward, inaugural GWS co-captain.

A lot of people don't realise that these whiteboards are as much for the coach as for the players – they're reminders of what you wanted to talk about.

TRUE MATES FOR A LIFETIME

PETER WARD AND I WENT TO SCHOOL TOGETHER, St Ignatius. We barracked for Richmond together; his old man, Snowy, was a trainer at Punt Road. Thankfully, for me at least, even though both our numbers came up in the days of National Service, I didn't go to Vietnam with Peter.

Most of my time in the army was spent at Puckapunyal, playing footy, peeling spuds and conducting all sorts of experiments with explosives. There was no experimenting where Peter was. At Nui Dat he got to see the real thing, and to photograph it.

Peter's fellow Vietnam vets remember him as a good bloke, and a good soldier. Because he had already started work as an apprentice photographer at the *Herald* and the *Weekly Times* when he was called up, the Army put him in the press corp. He saw the best and worst of war: the mateship that is an essential part of Australian military history; bodies of fallen comrades.

He might have been an apprentice photographer when he joined the army, but he quickly became a master of his craft. Peter's works – including both still and moving images, and moving in every sense – are part of the Australian War Memorial's National Collection. The best of them are portraits, capturing the expressions of young men confronted by all that war is and desperately trying to understand it; they probably never really did. As Peter said so often, 'Geez, we were kids, what did we know?'

One of his most famous pictures was that of Sergeant Peter Buckney from the Royal Australian Regiment's 8th Battalion. Buckney's daughter paid tribute to Peter Ward when he died after the last of his battles, with cancer, at the age of 67.

She wrote: 'RIP sir, you and your work showed the absolute truth of what my father and others endured in Nam. Your work will always be filtered through the generations to come. Thank you for your dedication and amazing photography under such horrific conditions. Respectfully, Tracee Buckney.'

Happily, photography took Peter to a lot of places apart from Vietnam: he covered Olympic Games, a pinnacle for any

With Peter's dad, Snowy (Ron) Ward, who was a trainer at Richmond for 28 years. The whole Ward family have meant so much to me, and have been a huge part of my life.

photographer – though it could also have been a personal sporting pinnacle. In 1968 he was half a chance to box for Australia at the Mexico Olympics as the Victorian amateur featherweight champion. Vietnam ended his boxing career, but it turned him into a heavyweight champion as a photographer, one good enough to win Walkley Awards.

I love Peter's footy photos, but he could turn his lens to other sports with equal success, and he was a brilliant general news snapper. Who else but Peter could have convinced Mick Gatto to let him into his fortress and photograph the celebrations after being acquitted of the murder of Andrew 'Benji' Veniamin?

Because Peter and I were school mates going back forever, there was always a special bond between us. At press conferences we'd give each other a little look and smile that said, 'Hello again.' That's just how it is when your lives are shared all the way back to the days at St Ignatius.

Peter appeared in a photo that is a special memory for me. It is us together at the MCG when I was coach of Greater Western Sydney. I wrote a little dedication on it:

My St Ignatius team mate – 1956
For Life
To my legend of a mate
Love having a life with you

Peter's funeral was held at St Ignatius Church. His life was celebrated at the place where we had become friends for the first time – and a lifetime. ●

In 2015 I lost a great friend in Peter Ward. A brilliant photographer, featherweight boxing champion of Victoria and a Vietnam vet. Here we are together at my 372nd – and last – game at the 'G. It was gratifying to share it with a mate.

If Mike Pyke, a Canadian rugby player, can play in a premiership for the Swans, Israel Folau could play in a premiership for the Giants. Not many AFL coaches coach and develop a rugby player for the nation, so I was fortunate to be one of them. Folau is a wonderful athlete, a true gentleman, and he would have made it in AFL if he'd stayed. To ask him to play in the youngest and least experienced side in history and expect him to become a champion was enormous.

Putting people at ease

I've been lucky to have had some excellent coaches in my time, spread across three forms of football in Rugby League, Rugby Union and the AFL. In Rugby League I had Mal Meninga with Queensland and Craig Bellamy at Melbourne Storm, and I definitely put Kevin Sheedy up with those two.

Each had a huge impact on my career, but Sheeds's role was different in that he was teaching me a game from scratch. Kevin always made me feel comfortable, building the belief that I could make the transition. Towards the end of my two years at the Giants, I saw him less as a coach and more as a friend and father figure, and to me that's what a good coach is all about. I need to know that my coaches care about me and are genuinely interested in what sort of person I am, which in my case is easy-going – I like to keep things simple. When I have that sort of relationship with a coach, I will give them everything I've got.

I did that for Kevin. He had already been signed to the Giants when I came over from Rugby League, and the opportunity to learn from him was a big part of my decision to leave Rugby League. He was very good at keeping things simple. There would be a thousand things going through my head as I was trying to learn all these new skills and then execute them in a game, but he would just say, 'Relax, you'll get there, just back your instincts. If you get in the clear, just go for it as if you were playing Rugby League.'

That took away the fear of making a mistake, and if I did make a mistake he would find the positive in it, which was also helpful because I have high standards: if I do ten good things and one bad thing, I tend to focus on the bad thing. One *very* good thing was the game against the Gold Coast in Canberra. It was special to have played a role in the club's first win and to get to sing the club song.

Winning is something the Giants do a lot these days, and I did have a laugh when they made the finals for the first time and Kevin suggested it was time to bring me back to the AFL. But the laugh became a smile, because I was reminded of all the support he had given me. He was arguing that I had struggled to learn the game in such a young team, but that now they were all mature players, I would find the transition easier. We won't find out if he's right, but it was typical of the things Kevin comes out with – sometimes to get a headline, sometimes to break the ice or have a bit of fun. He has a good balance between football and the rest of life, and I think that was why he had a good relationship with all the nervous new Giants players.

Kevin taught me things that I have carried over to Rugby Union with the Waratahs and the Wallabies. He taught me about owning the ball in the air, which really sharpened up my marking skills. I refined a lot of things at the Giants, especially my awareness around the football. He was a great teacher, but more importantly he is a great person, and I will always have plenty of time for what he has done for me and for sport.

Israel Folau, Australian representative Rugby League and Rugby Union player and inaugural AFL Giant.

Moving on after four years of coaching GWS. Those young players were fantastic, and brave – leaving the security of home to start a whole new club. As the game moves on they will not be forgotten.

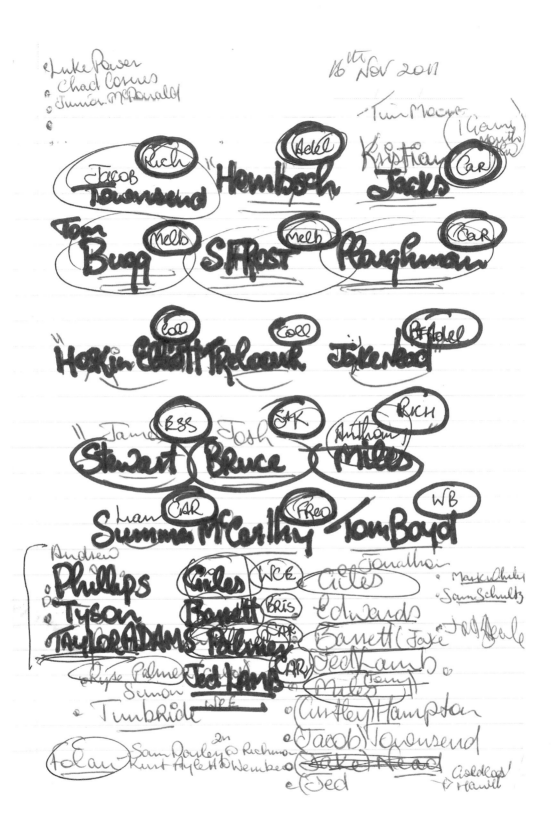

The team that was cleared from the Giants in the first five years – Victorian clubs, stop your whinging!

Winding up the siren in 2017 as I reprise my signature tune. They wrote a song about it: 'Wave wave your jacket and stick it up the Eagles.'

10
RETURN TO ESSENDON

Ah it's great to be back among friends and, in my 50th year of senior footy, to be getting paid to 'innovate'! It makes me appreciate all the more those Bomber people who stood by me as coach. Football is nothing without people, and those are some of the best people in footy.

BACK TO THE BOMBERS

HELLO, I'M BACK, DID YOU MISS ME?
In early 2013 there was this growing feeling that if ever there was a time to go back to Essendon, it was now. The challenges of Greater Western Sydney had been enjoyable, as had the Sydney lifestyle, but Essendon said it needed me, and I had to respond.

In March 2015 I returned to Essendon – not to coach, but to be General Manager, Commercial Development and Innovation.

The club was still working its way through the supplements saga. James Hird was coach, but each day he was coming under enormous pressure to resign. They got him in the end, though even that wouldn't stop the turmoil. It was no longer the Essendon of old, but it wasn't as bad as some people, particularly in the media, were making out. To me, we still had a great big bomber aeroplane sitting in that brand-new hangar out at Tullamarine, it

One of these photos is about loyalty, the other is about family. This painting was created for my 600th game. In the left photo are the board members and people who kept me at Essendon for 27 years; some, like the late great Ron Evans, are now deceased. On the right are the Sheedy family as well as great friend Steven Dring, a mad Tigers fan. There's also Garry and Lyn Fenech, all friends from my Prahran tech days.

just had a broken wing that needed mending.

We still don't know the full story of the supplements saga, and we may never know. I have just always thought it disgraceful that Dustin Fletcher, who wasn't involved in the program and was never drug tested, was punished to the extent that he could not even watch his children play sport.

Apart from feeling at home, another reason to be happy about being back at Essendon was Mark 'The Phantom' Doran, a very special person at the club who you can always rely on to boost morale in tough times. He has done that for himself all his life. When Mark was born with cerebral palsy, his wonderful parents, Rex and Barbara, were told not to expect him to live long. In 2017 he turned 60, and would have to be the most passionate Essendon supporter ever, rarely missing a training

session – during which he often gets to address the players. He is one of the best loved people at Essendon, and has been for over three or four decades – even though he could cause trouble from time to time.

Mark had 'access to all areas' at Essendon from well before I began coaching there. There was a time that club officials were tearing their hair out because Channel Seven seemed to know the details of the Essendon team at the same time as the coaches. It was thought that there must be a phantom around the club. When they finally worked out that it was Mark listening in on team selection and then ringing the Channel Seven sports team with the news, he was christened 'the Phantom'.

On the Thursday before the 1984 Grand Final, I got Mark to address the team after training and he was just fantastic. He spoke to players as a group and individually – he told Paul Vander Haar to go straight home after training and not to have a drink on the way – and he just worked magic with them, making them feel totally relaxed despite the tension of the week. When you know of people like Mark who have invested so much of their lives into the club, you know you just have to go back to do what you can, whether you're a player, coach or former coach with something to offer.

The fans, it's always about the fans. If we don't have them, young and old, we don't have a game.

When Kevin is on time ...

In 2016 I joined Kevin Sheedy on the ever-growing list of people who have written books about Australian football, calling mine *Bomber: The Whole Story*. When it hit the shelves, a friend told me that when he checked the index, the name Kevin Sheedy got more mentions than ASADA. I was pleased about that, because I am determined that the disgraceful way I was treated through the AFL-ASADA process will never define me, but I am forever happy to have my long-term association with Kevin Sheedy help to define me.

When I arrived at Essendon as a teenage hopeful, he was the coach. When I played in successive winning grand finals in 1984 and 1985, he was the coach. When I added another grand final in 1993 as a captain, he was the coach, and when I became an assistant coach with ambitions to become a senior coach, he was the coach.

When I finally became a senior coach, he was still the senior coach at Essendon, so I got coached by Kevin Sheedy, and I got to coach against him – including in his last year, which, while it might not have been a great time for him, was the best year of my football life – winning the 2007 premiership for the people of Geelong.

And guess what, after his time at Greater Western Sydney, in the year that he turns 70, he's still at Essendon – not as the coach, but with some fancy new title: General Manager, Commercial Development and Innovation. Innovation and Kevin Sheedy on the same business card, who would ever have thought that?

A great image for Australian tradies: an electrician (Bomber Thompson) and a plumber. I always said, make one mistake as a plumber and you get wet; make one mistake as an electrician and you're dead. When Bomber was considering a career switch, I pointed out that coaching was bound to be better than getting electrocuted.

Some people might think this comes into the category of too much information, but his wonderful mum, Irene, once said that while he played with Prahran and Richmond, he was always Essendon, because that was where he was conceived. When the time comes for him to go up to heaven – and Kevin, I hope it is a long way off – I reckon he will still be wearing black and red wherever he goes, because everyone knows what Kevin has done over the years to promote the Essendon Football Club, to make it the juggernaut that it is.

He's also been the best salesman that Australian Rules Football has ever seen – around Australia, around the world – but what a lot of people might not know is the impact that Kevin has had on the lives of those with whom he's come into contact. So many of his players have been influenced by Kevin, not just in the way they play football, but in the way they go about the whole of their lives: it's the way Kevin can look you in the eye and ask you a question like, 'Are you happy?' and it makes you really think about what you are doing in your life.

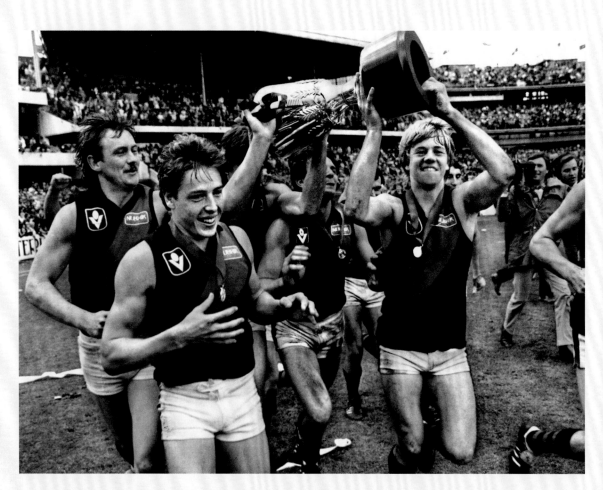

The silent man of Essendon, Gary Foulds, with the cup. A wonderful schoolteacher and parent who had 300 games at Bomberland. Here he's running around with two baby Bombers, the youngest players on the ground: Bomber Thompson and Mark Harvey, who both became coaches later.

I think he does that because people like Graeme Richmond, Tommy Hafey and Harry Beitzel did the same thing for him when he was playing at Richmond, always encouraging him to get the best out of himself. When he asks you the questions, and you responded positively, he gives you more encouragement – and more responsibility. He made me captain because he liked the fact that, though still in my 20s, I was running my own business in partnership with my brother. He jokes that he thought I'd be a good captain because I was an electrician. Electricians must be very careful in everything they do because one mistake and *pow*, you're gone, whereas if you're a plumber and you stuff up, all that happens is you get covered with the yucky stuff.

Kevin is very generous, as he was to me when I first went to coach Geelong in 2000, a time when the club was broke. He agreed to do a 'sportie' to help raise money, even though we probably weren't as close as we had been when I was playing at Essendon. There was also the fact I was now a rival coach, so why would he do anything to help me and my new club? But there he was that night, up on the podium, giving his time for free, and any issues between us disappeared. He said, 'You know we've probably spent more time in each other's company than we have with our wives?' I replied, 'So we should have at least three kids,' and the audience loved it.

We had a team of kids in 1993 when we won the flag at Essendon, and even though we were young, I had already sensed we might be onto something special that year – you always knew that when Kevin was on time for training and taking

it all very seriously, you had a chance of winning the flag. Kevin being on time! I think his body runs to a completely different clock to everyone else. He has other faults too, like the way he could muck around with the team when we were in front, playing blokes out of position, that sort of thing – though he will tell you he was only trying to develop the players, or to learn more about them. When I became a coach I had a better understanding of that, and plenty of the other burdens that senior coaches carry.

It's not until you do the job that you really understand just what a full-on challenge being the senior coach is, because you have the role of leading not just the players but the whole club, keeping up morale, restoring confidence, keeping the members on-side, keeping the board on-side. There is one thing I saw Kevin do that I hope I never have to do, and that is to speak at the funeral of one of my premiership players, as Sheeds had to do when Nobby Clarke died. We were all sitting there bawling our eyes out, including Kevin. Then he got up, gave this eulogy that did Nobby proud, and then sat down and started crying again with the rest of us.

That I did well enough to win two flags as a senior coach at Geelong is in a big part down to many things I learned from Kevin, the ones that made him a genius and the ones that frustrated me too. He can still do that, frustrate people, but I still say, enjoy Kevin Sheedy while you can, because there will never be anyone like him again.

Mark Thompson, three-time premiership player and two-time premiership coach.

WORKING FOR FOOTY

IF BEING AROUND THE CLUB AND AVAILABLE TO fans helps sustain morale around Essendon, then I'm delighted to contribute, but there's plenty more to do. The club were pioneers in creating blockbuster occasions like the Anzac Day clash and Dreamtime at the 'G, and we were keen to add another.

The seed for the Country Game had already been sewn. On a visit to Wagga Wagga a few years earlier I had been moved by the terrible stories of hardship in the bush, and of farmers taking their own lives. I kept hearing them in other parts of Australia too, from people in communities that felt like they were being forgotten. We needed to find a way to show them they hadn't been. We had found a way to honour our soldiers and the first Australians through two football games, and I thought we should do the same for our country kin.

Now, a lot of folk from that part of the world think of Geelong as a great, big grown-up city with its own university and brand-new boutique sports stadium, but through the Western District it had a deep connection with farmers, so we went to the Cats and asked them if they wanted to be part of a third blockbuster. Their CEO, Brian Cook, said yes, and we are starting to get the message out all over Australia that city people do care about their cousins in the bush – and not just the farmers. The emergency workers and the firefighters in particular were an important part of it all.

In May 2017 Brian Cook and I were auctioned off at a fundraiser for another wonderful group of people working with Australian farmers: Brian Egan and Aussie Helpers. Someone thought having dinner with Brian and me was worth $3200.

Over the entrée I thought I might just pick Brian's brain about how you arrive at a club that's bankrupt in 1999, and by 2017 have three premierships, three Brownlow Medallists, a brand-new Brownlow Stand that cost $91 million and not much debt. When you hear some of the other clubs whinging about all the concessions that GWS and the Suns received, you should ask why they can't do what Geelong – and Hawthorn – have done over the past decades. Hawthorn almost merged with Melbourne in 1996. Now it's the most successful club of the past ten years.

There's another ambition for the Bombers: that is to be the first club with 100,000 members. Hopefully more and more of those members will come from outside Australia. We already have the Orange County Bombers in California, and India is a great place to take Australian football. There are many big cricket stadiums like the one in Trivandrum, home of the Kerala Bombers. Those Bombers were keen – they made a four-and-a-half flight to Kolkata for the Indian AFL national championships. They played in matches all day and were still going at kick-to-kick in the dark.

The Giants in Kolkata in 2017. It's exciting to see our game spreading across the world, and India is a perfect place to focus on. Indian people have natural attributes for footy, and these kids had already started to build a passion for it by watching the game on YouTube.

Another thing I'd like to see is a return to State of Origin. In 1977 Leon Larkin, the marketing manager for the Subiaco Football Club, gave our game a huge head start against Rugby League when he organised a match between Victoria and Western Australia. State of Origin let players like Barry Cable and Max Richardson, who were playing in the VFL, play for their home state, and they thrashed the Victorians. In 1989, a huge 92,000 people watched Victoria play South Australia at the MCG, but then people in authority began to feel that since we had a national league, we didn't need any more interstate games.

We literally *gave* this wonderful marketing opportunity to Rugby League – it was Allen Aylett, the former head of the VFL, who suggested State of Origin to Queensland senator Ron McAuliffe. McAuliffe liked the idea that 'you can't take Queensland out of

the Queenslander' so much he pushed for the concept in Rugby League.

A great way to bring back State of Origin would be to revisit 1977 with a game between Victoria and Western Australia at the opening of the new Perth Stadium. You can take the West Australian out of Western Australia, but you can't take Western Australia out of the West Australian. Hello, Mitchell White! 🏉

OPPOSITE: The most important thing you must learn to do in football is to listen.

TOP RIGHT: Keeping track of pre-season grand final attendances. I've always taken the pre-season seriously. If you're in it, you're in it to win everything – Graeme Richmond taught me that. The crowds for these pre-season games are better than some of our home and away games, which should show how important they are. This should be where the AFL experiments with the best way to move our game into the future, to make it dominant – please take it seriously!

BOTTOM: Son of a gun, Jobe Watson, from a great Essendon family. His father, Tim, did a great job as MC at the dinner to celebrate my 50 years in the VFL/AFL. You see them as teenagers and they turn into wonderful men and fathers.

Now that I'm back at Essendon, it's nice to get a chance to reflect on the big moments for the club that I've been lucky enough to be a part of. Working with this team, who won the 1985 premiership, was a real privilege. No matter where their careers took them, every person in this photo has remained part of the Essendon spirit.

Welcome back, boys. A reunion of the 1984/85 premiership side. Legendary players from Essendon's winning premiership, back 30 years later – look at Salmon up the back, he still dwarfs everyone!

My first crop of flowers. That bush is still going years later, and it's a monster now. I watered it at 7am this morning.

11

LIFE OUTSIDE FOOTBALL

Family, photography, travel, Australia, Walt Disney and a horse called Bel Esprit. Gaining and passing on knowledge, and being in nature. Stay close to nature and you can't go wrong. These are a few of my favourite things.

TIME TO DAYDREAM

WHEN YOU ARE DEEP INSIDE THE FOOTBALL bubble, you can forget there is a life outside it. That happens to a lot of people, especially some in Melbourne who don't seem to know that there is a whole country out there called Australia, and it sits at the bottom of a great big planet. One of my biggest interests outside football is getting to know the world, visiting places and hearing the stories of the history and the people, sometimes taking their ideas and seeing how they can be incorporated into my own life. Listening to people is one reason I am sometimes late for meetings. Daydreaming is another.

You need daydreaming time in your life, and sometimes if the daydream is a good one, you might not want to wake up. I love flying because it's the perfect time to daydream, when you're up there with your head in the clouds, alone with your thoughts and aspirations. I take lots of photos through the plane's window to remind me to keep daydreaming when I'm back on the ground.

Gardening is great for daydreaming too. The roses don't complain if you take a bit longer to get to them. I love the garden at our home in Melbourne. I get a lot of ideas for it by looking at other people's gardens, particularly the beautifully thought-out and maintained ones we had at Breakfast Point in Sydney. No doubt there's a gardener out there echoing the words of Tom Hafey when I left Richmond: 'He's taken everything that wasn't nailed down.'

I'm also fond of reflection, and I think it's valuable to look back on your decisions – to feel satisfied with the good decisions and to learn from the bad ones. Our leaders don't seem to be very good at that. How much have we learned from the decision to spend $43 million on the bid for the soccer World Cup for one pathetic vote? It's made worse by the fact the nation that was awarded the event, Qatar, has been ostracised by the rest of their Middle Eastern neighbours for supporting terrorism. Why spend all that money inviting a game to our shores when they're not even interested?

I know as well as anyone the satisfaction of seeing a game you love expand into new territory, but proper reflection will help you judge whether it's a worthwhile risk or whether it's just going to send you backwards. 🏈

TOP: The lake at the Royal Botanic Gardens in Melbourne, one of my favourite places in the world (although I fell in it after my first communion). I go there all the time. Most people walk like robots around the Tan, which loops around the edges. But I don't see the point – I prefer to walk in and through the gardens.

RIGHT: The garden patrol out putting trees in.

TOP LEFT: Mid-1990s. I never told Geraldine and the kids we were going to walk up Kosciusko, or even that I had a hotel booked. I just pulled in at night when we were travelling through the region. They had to climb to the highest point of Australia whether they liked it or not, because I had the car keys and they weren't going anywhere till we'd made it. They loved it in the end.

TOP MIDDLE: One of my best travel experiences, visiting the Ellis Island museum in New York. I really got an insight into migration to America compared to Australia. The US took in 10 million people over a decade; that's an amazing thing to happen to a country. And you could find every family's name in an electronic history. Made me think that in Australia we are too slow and disorganised, and we don't learn from history. This is too big an island for only 25 million people. How slow can you go?

TOP RIGHT: Narooma, NSW. Where else in the world would you find a rock cut by the ocean into the (near) shape of Australia?

BOTTOM LEFT: At the top of Kosciusko on another trip with Michael Long and Che Cockatoo-Collins.

BOTTOM MIDDLE: My first European holiday with the family: England, Ireland, Scotland and France. It was a great trip that opened our eyes to class and culture.

BOTTOM RIGHT: Mum's first ever trip to the snow, at the bottom of the Grand Canyon in the early 1990s.

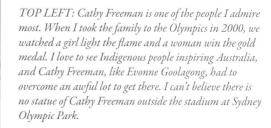

TOP LEFT: Cathy Freeman is one of the people I admire most. When I took the family to the Olympics in 2000, we watched a girl light the flame and a woman win the gold medal. I love to see Indigenous people inspiring Australia, and Cathy Freeman, like Evonne Goolagong, had to overcome an awful lot to get there. I can't believe there is no statue of Cathy Freeman outside the stadium at Sydney Olympic Park.

TOP MIDDLE: Muhammad Ali, the greatest athlete of all time. He was a magnificent, entertaining boxer – a boxer rather than a fighter, there are big differences. What he achieved was mind-boggling.

TOP RIGHT: Why wouldn't you want Kylie Minogue's autograph? A girl who really hit the world. She was given a good life by her parents and worked hard to do something with it.

MIDDLE LEFT: Two superstars I worked with over the years: Harry Beitzel, a great mentor on radio, and Sam Newman, probably the most generous TV celebrity I've ever met.

MIDDLE: If only it was the real Walt Disney: the world's best 'happiness coach'. I've always admired him for the fun and joy he's given the world, and the best conference I've ever attended, by the length and breadth of Australia, was in Disney World in Florida. Disney doesn't get enough credit, and I think of him as the opposite to all the evil people who've influenced the world – Hitler, Pol Pot, Stalin. It's happiness versus evil, so let's celebrate happiness more.

MIDDLE RIGHT: Meeting Bear Grylls. I love his passion for his show – an amazing young man.

BOTTOM LEFT: The great Pat Cash in his Hawthorn guernsey, on a tour of Britain and Ireland.

BOTTOM MIDDLE: Our last prime minister worth his salt – not much has been done since. I also liked Keating. There are two types of politician: those who have a vision and those who don't.

BOTTOM RIGHT: Not sure how I made it onto Warnie's phone. I'd say he was just slightly better than me at bowling – at least he turned the ball. To raise money for charity with Sheedyvision, we made bats called LBW (Lillee, Bradman and Warne), and it was one of the best things we did.

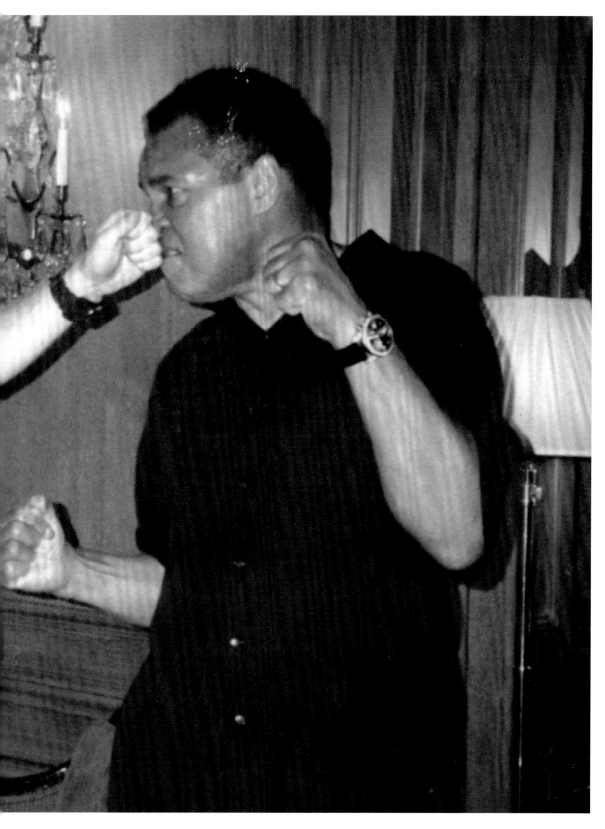

I have over 50,000 photos on my phone and iPad, but this one is my absolute favourite. Taken at the Four Seasons Hotel in LA, the legendary Muhammad Ali sparring with my son, Samuel Thomas Sheedy.

BACKING A WINNER

HORSE RACING HAS ALWAYS BEEN A GREAT way for me to get away from football. Ever since my dad took me to the races as a young fella, I have loved studying the form guide and having a punt – not the only footballer to do that. Back in the days when race results were put up on the old manual scoreboards, blokes like Polly Farmer would pull the form guide out of their socks mid-game to see how their tips were going.

Another thing about going to the races that made it different from football was that I could just go as a fan with no other involvement, though that changed a bit when I was fortunate enough to be included in a syndicate that owned Bel Esprit, a horse whose pedigree goes back to the legendary stallion Nijinsky and forward to one of the greatest horses Australia has ever produced: Black Caviar. In many ways, it was the completion of a circle that began when I went with Mal Brown to Kentucky to see Nijinsky in 1974. That would be the same Mal Brown who missed the 1974 Grand Final because of suspension; on that Kentucky trip, after a few drinks, he reckons he found me kissing and cuddling a lamp post. I thought she had cold lips.

It was a couple of other old friends who got me involved in the Bel Esprit syndicate. Michael Duffy, a former Minister in the Hawke government and a huge Essendon supporter who has long been involved in racing, had invited Brian Donohoe to be part of the syndicate. Brian said to Michael that he thought there was one name missing from the list: mine. Michael agreed.

I certainly got a kick out of watching Bel Esprit win the Blue Diamond Stakes and some other big races before heading off to stud, where I'm sure he got a kick out of setting a record of 264 coverings in one season. Because of equine flu, Bel Esprit was just about the only stallion with any decent pedigree in Victoria.

Black Caviar wasn't among that 264. She came along a bit later to produce one of the greatest winning streaks in the history of Australian racing – unbeaten in 25 races. Because of the Bel Esprit connection, we got to hear about her very early in her career, and watched her reputation grow with pride. ●

TOP: Horsing around on a statue of Black Caviar at Rick Jamieson's property on Lake Nagambie. Seeing as Bel Esprit was Black Caviar's sire, I thought it was a good opportunity for a photo. Unfortunately, I didn't consider how hot a statue like this might get in the sunshine. I couldn't sit down again for days.

BOTTOM: Bel Esprit was the busiest sire in the world in 2007 because of Equine Influenza – 264 coverings. Before he went to stud, he won a few good races.

Samuel Johnson in the back pocket

In 2017 Kevin Sheedy was presented with the Vicsport Outstanding Contribution to Sport Award, and I had the honour of announcing him as the winner in front of a crowd of 1000 people at an event at the Melbourne Exhibition Centre. To get Kevin there, he had been told by his executive assistant, Jeanette Curwood – the woman without whom he would never get anywhere – that he was going to be a member of panel conversation and was to just sit in the audience until the MC called him up onto the stage. Instead of calling him up, though, the MC said that there would now be a special presentation, which was my cue to come on stage.

Without naming him, I outlined the person who was the subject of this special presentation; his playing career, his coaching career and the great social change he had achieved in Australia through football, and then announced that the winner of the Victorian Sports Achievement Award was Kevin John Sheedy.

> Startled, he got up from his seat, made his way up on stage, pointed one of his gnarled fingers at me and said, 'I will get you for this.'

There was still more to come. As he was ushered to the side of the stage to have his photo taken with various dignitaries, his family quietly made their way onto the stage. When he turned around and saw Geraldine, the children, their partners, and his new grandson, Tom, he burst into tears. Richmond's tough number 10, Essendon's ruthless, roaring coach, burst into tears. Family means a lot to Kevin.

I knew of Kevin long before I knew him. I was at the SCG in 1987 when Sydney beat Essendon by 27 goals and I was in the stands at North Hobart Oval in 1992 when Essendon beat Fitzroy by three points. But it wasn't until 1997, after moving to Melbourne to work as a football writer for *The Australian*, that I met Kevin. My sons barracked for Essendon so I thought I would impress them by interviewing Kevin. We met at the Jack & Jill cafe in Napier Street, and before I had a chance to switch on my tape recorder, he got in first with a question: 'What do you think of the idea of back men kicking the ball across the goal to each other?' This was something that was still new in the game. I said, 'What, like they do in hockey, until they find the opening they want to go forward?'

There was this flicker in his eyes; I don't know whether he thought 'smartarse' or that this bloke might have some ideas he could steal, remembering what Tommy Hafey said when Kevin left Richmond. It might have been the latter, because, and I didn't know this, Kevin was negotiating to write a column for *The Australian* – the national daily. He liked the idea of being able to talk to all of Australia and asked for me to be

The best gotcha ever – I thought I was guest speaking that night! It took a long time, but they finally got me. I may be slipping.

After being well and truly stitched up. I don't know if I can ever believe anything Geraldine tells me again.

OPPOSITE and ABOVE: 'Before and after'. My executive assistant, Jeanette Curwood, has been there half of my 50 years in football. A great relationship.

his ghost writer. I must say, I wasn't all that enthusiastic; I'd heard the stories of other ghost writers who would hide under desks when he came into their newspaper offices to write his columns, and the one who was often reduced to tears because he couldn't find Kevin when deadline was approaching.

Kevin's thoughts can be quite exotic when you do get hold of him, and getting them into black and white can be like herding cats, so you'd always want to read them back to him, but he'd disappear again. He missed a few deadlines, but I just hit the send button anyway and there were never any complaints. I've lost count of the number of columns we've written that way. I once said I was James Boswell to his Samuel Johnson, and he asked which team they played in the back pocket for, adding in that Leprechaun-like way of his, 'Did you like that?' Another time I said that being taught about Australian football by him was like learning how to paint a ceiling from Michelangelo. He liked that.

Kevin has also been very generous to my family, even acting as a referee for my sons when they were looking to rent houses. It's amazing how responsive real estate agents become when they see Kevin's name at the bottom of an application. Two agents in Northcote almost came to blows over who would call to check out the reference. The boys have never missed out on a house or flat.

Warwick Hadfield, Sports Editor, ABC Radio National Breakfast, and Kevin's long-term amanuensis.

ABOVE: With Mum and Geraldine, receiving the Order of Australia in Melbourne's Government House, right in our own backyard in South Yarra.

LEFT: Receiving a doctorate from the University of Western Sydney – a very humbling experience. It's great that whenever I give advice to any of my medical doctors, I can send them an account from Dr Sheedy for the same price they charge me (which, by the way, is nothing).

ABOVE: My 50th birthday present was a ride on a Harley.

LEFT: My fourth brother, John, the cowboy of the club. He could be anywhere in Australia at any time – your typical gypsy, every family has one.

OPPOSITE TOP: The Sheedy clan, all of Irene and Tom's grandkids.

OPPOSITE BOTTOM: Me and my sister Kathy do share a resemblance. When I went down the Big Freeze slide in the wig everyone thought it was her.

Three beautiful daughters even more beautiful at their weddings. Geraldine and I were bursting with pride on each of these special days.

Charlotte and Oliver, and me with baby Thomas Kevin. They are great fun, the kids. I'm probably having more time with my grandkids than I did with my own kids at that age. Charlotte is determined to marry the captain of Essendon – Dyson Heppell is being haunted and hunted by my granddaughter.

WORDS OF WISDOM

SOME MIGHT SUGGEST THAT I LIKE THE SOUND of my own voice, but it is true that I like public speaking. Whatever the forum – whether I'm talking to people in business, in a sporting club, or some other group – it's always an honour to be able to pass on some of the knowledge that other people have given me. Having said that, the people in the Australian Olympic Committee might not be too happy about the time in 2006 when Ric Charlesworth, the hockey superstar, and I went to Warwickshire in England to talk to British coaches – not with the way Great Britain's Olympic medal tally has gone compared to Australia's.

A wonderful promoter on the public speaking circuit was my friend – the world's friend, really – Richard Custerson, who died in 2016. Dickie Boy was forever organising sportsmen's nights with people like Ian Botham, Max Walker, Dermott Brereton – all the big names. And everyone just loved him, particularly the people up the bush to whom he brought these legends. He had his own mission statement, a hand-written one, which was included on the program for his funeral service. I think it's worth sharing:

'My Mission Statement: To thank God and acknowledge him for the wonderful gifts he has given me. A wonderful family to cherish and to build a loving, healthy environment to develop and grow them. Always be cheerful and happy and to love life. Communicate and respect people of all walks of life. To lead and show strength, to always do the right thing and treat people with kindness and respect. To enjoy and love life!'

Beautiful words, particularly those about family. Geraldine and I have four children: Renee, Chelsea, Jessica and Sam, all good kids. Renee has two children, Charlotte and Oliver Kevin; Chelsea has Tom. I reckon up there in heaven, my parents, Tom and Irene, are smiling, nudging each another and saying, 'We didn't do too badly, did we?'

And that other Tom who joined them in 2014, Tom Hafey – he's probably sipping on a heavenly cup of tea and conceding I haven't done too badly considering I was 'nothing but a back-pocket plumber'. Another moment of recognition here on Earth was being given the Vicsport Outstanding Contribution to Sport Award for 2016 – a great honour, but also one of the biggest stitch-ups in my life. I will get Warwick Hadfield back for that one day.

I'm in the final quarter of my life now, looking back to the little boy sitting in his classroom gazing out at the MCG, or the young footballer nursing a bung knee in 1967 and worried that his football career had already come to an end, and I can think, it's all gone pretty well – so far.

I intend to cram as much into the final quarter as we did when we kicked a record 11 goals against Hawthorn in the 1985 grand final: helping Essendon grow, helping the AFL grow, watching Bel Esprit's family grow, watching my own prosper. Wherever that takes me, well, who knows, but as I go I will keep singing along with Roy Rogers:

Don't fence me in.

It was great to work with my dear friend Dick Custerson and his event management company, A Positive Move, helping young people starting out in business and encouraging them to keep moving forward.

SHEEDY'S TEAM OF THE HALF-CENTURY

'HARD', THAT'S THE WORD TO DESCRIBE PICKING MY best team of the past 50 years of VFL and AFL football. Hard because there were a lot of great players from which to choose and some very talented footballers had to be left out, and hard because when it came down to the final decisions, I drew on my experience at Richmond and Essendon and went for players who were always hardest at the ball. I could have picked 'Superboot', Bernie Quinlan, but the forwards I did eventually go with were that little bit tougher. No one has ever been harder than Leigh Matthews – ask Barrie Robran or the point post at Windy Hill.

Mick Malthouse couldn't find a spot for one Ablett in his best 25 of the past 50 years. I've got two. When you were hit by Gary Ablett Senior, you stayed that way. Paul Brown, who played 84 games for Geelong, tells a story of being tagged by an opponent, and Gary Ablett Senior said, 'Brownie, is that bloke annoying you?' Paul replied yes. 'Just walk him past me,' said Ablett senior. Paul did as instructed. Next thing there was great sound of air leaving someone's lungs, and the tagger was on the ground. Ablett Senior was a cruel bastard, and

he could kick goals – 14 of them in one day against Essendon. Gary Ablett Junior is also an exceptional player, a little more consistent than his father, but no less explosive.

In the ruck, Simon Madden was one of the easiest players to pick, the best ever and full of the courage you need to jump for the ball, exposing your chest and abdomen to your opponent's knee. Michael Voss and Kevin Bartlett would have had a ball running off him.

Down back, Gavin Wanganeen and Dustin Fletcher have earned their spots, and I just went for David Dench ahead of Stephen Silvagni at fullback.

It took a while to work out who I wanted at centre halfback. It was very tempting to go for 'The Sundance Kid', Paul Roos. In the end, though, Peter Knights is the right choice.

Mark Ricciuto gets on the bench because he was a tough little pest for the Adelaide Crows who would drive you mad. James Hird is probably best remembered for his class and silky skills but he was also as hard at the ball as they come. Remember he twice came back from injury, the second a serious

I ran out of options that day he kicked 14 on us – thankfully we had Paul Salmon at the other end. Gary Ablett Senior was one of the toughest people to play against because he had great strength, a low centre of gravity, and he loved getting the ball.

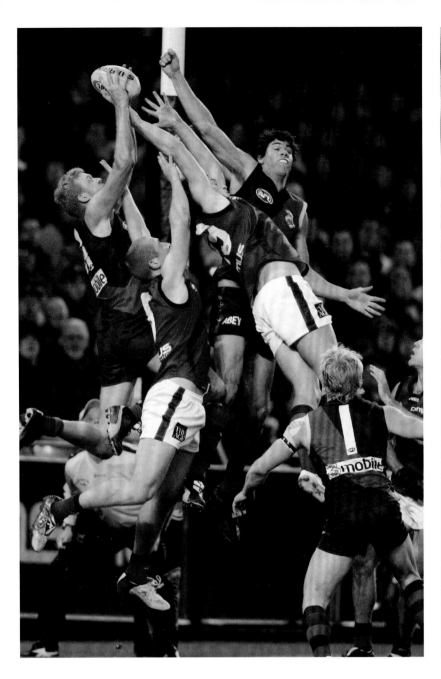

one to his face, and the first moment of the first game back he straightaway put his head over the ball. That's courage; that's the sort of hardness that coaches love.

As well as being another hard footballer, I just love Jason Dunstall's amazing 1000-goal journey from Coorparoo, Queensland to the MCG on grand final day. He can be rude

these days, and you don't have to like him, but there's no doubt Hawthorn found their own Wally Lewis in Jason.

As always with these teams, they're only a great way to start the discussion. When picking your best team of the past 50 years, put together a longlist of people with skills, then go for the hardest. Discuss.

LEFT: Dustin Fletcher, 400 games. A true son of Essendon from a great Bomber family, his father, Ken, is one of the best people I have met in football.

RIGHT: I don't think Leigh Matthews has ever forgiven Essendon for winning that grand final in 1985, the last game of his career. Maybe including him in my Team of the Half Century will change that.

TEAM OF THE HALF-CENTURY

FULLBACK

GAVIN WANGANEEN
300 games, 2 flags, 1 Brownlow Medal, 1 B&F, 5 All Australian teams

DAVID DENCH
275 games, 2 flags, 4 B&F

DUSTIN FLETCHER
400 games, 2 flags, 1 B&F, 2 All Australian teams

HALFBACK

BRUCE DOULL
356 games, 4 flags, 4 B&F 2 All Australian teams, 1 Norm Smith Medal

PETER KNIGHTS
264 games, 3 flags, 2 B&F

COREY ENRIGHT
332 games, 3 flags, 2 B&F 6 All Australian teams

CENTRE

FRANCIS BOURKE
300 games, 5 flags, 1 B&F

IAN STEWART
205 games, 2 flags, 3 Brownlow Medals, 3 B&F, 1 All Australian team

JASON AKERMANIS
325 games, 3 flags, 1 Brownlow Medal, 2 B&F, 4 All Australian teams

HALF-FORWARD

ROYCE HART
187 games, 4 flags, 2 B&F 1 All Australian team

WAYNE CAREY
272 games, 2 flags, 4 B&F 7 All Australian teams

GARY ABLETT SENIOR
248 games, 1 B&F 9 All Australian teams, 1 Norm Smith Medal

FULL-FORWARD

LEIGH MATTHEWS
332 games, 4 flags, 8 B&F 3 All Australian teams

TONY LOCKETT
281 games, 1 Brownlow Medal, 3 B&F, 6 All Australian teams

GARY ABLETT JUNIOR
300+ games, 2 flags, 2 Brownlow Medals, 5 B&F, 8 All Australian teams

RUCKS

SIMON MADDEN
378 games, 2 flags, 4 B&F
10 All Australian teams, 1 Norm
Smith Medal

MICHAEL VOSS
289 games, 3 flags, 1 Brownlow
Medal, 5 B&F, 5 All Australian teams

KEVIN BARTLETT
403 games, 5 flags, 5 B&F,
1 Norm Smith Medal

BENCH

JOHN NICHOLLS
328 games, 3 flags, 5 B&F
2 All Australian teams

MARK RICCIUTO
312 games, 1 flag, 1 Brownlow
Medal, 3 B&F, 8 All Australian teams

JAMES HIRD
253 games, 2 flags, 1 Brownlow
Medal, 5 B&F, 5 All Australian
teams, 1 Norm Smith Medal

CHRIS JUDD
279 games, 1 flag, 2 Brownlow
Medals, 5 B&F, 6 All Australian teams
1 Norm Smith Medal

BOBBY SKILTON
237 games, 3 Brownlow Medals,
9 B&F

JASON DUNSTALL
269 games, 4 flags, 4 B&F,
4 All Australian teams

COACH

TOM HAFEY
522 games, 10 grand finals, 4 flags,
66 per cent win record

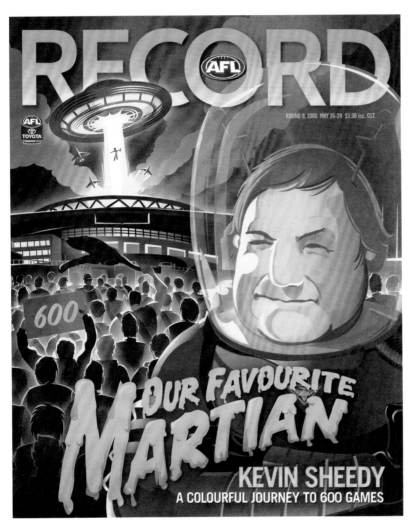

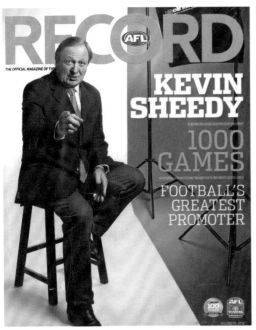

TOP: *A celebration for my 600th VFL/AFL game. Through my whole working life I referred to the umpires as 'Martians', and it was clearly a favourite comment for the public and the press. I always thought Mars should have asked me to do some ads for them – it's never too late.*

BOTTOM: *Very proud to be able to sit and talk about helping the game with the* Record*. The game has been my life, and many people have helped to push it into the future.*

OPPOSITE: *A picture by artist Geoff Naismith: all mixed up, a life member of three AFL clubs. The question I'm asked most is, 'Who do you barrack for?' The answer is I can't put my wife ahead of my daughters, ahead of my son – everyone's important.*

BOOKS LIKE THIS ONE DON'T MAKE IT TO THE shelves without a genuine team effort.

The staff at Affirm Press were a crucial part of the team: Keiran Rogers, Ruby Ashby-Orr, Grace Breen, Karen Wallis, Cosima McGrath, Nicole McKenzie, Emily Ashenden and Stephanie Bishop-Hall – and last but by no means least, Martin Hughes.

Martin's choice of a football team is a bit of a worry – the Bulldogs. He tried to get me to pick Teddy Whitten in my team of the half-century. His loyalties also explain why he insisted on having a piece from Callan Ward in the book. He still hasn't got over us whisking him out of Footscray to a life of luxury at Breakfast Point in Sydney.

A big thank you to all the people who have written chapters for the book. I don't think we need to get the lawyers involved.

Special thanks to these people and organisations for helping with the images: Ondrej Folton from News Limited, who went above and beyond to help us source photos; Gregor McCaskie and Friends of EFC; Roland Weekes and the Richmond FC; GWS Media Department; Michael Lovett and the AFL Media Department; Kevin Sheehan at the AFL for the International Rules photographs; Michael Dodge; Bruno Cannatelli; and the Victorian Sport Awards.

Some of those photos were provided by members of my family, my brothers and sisters and my wife, Geraldine, with assistance from our children. Thanks for helping – it is as much your story as mine.

Thanks to Warwick Hadfield for helping with the words again. It's been a great partnership since our first meeting in Windy Hill 20 years ago. It's nice to have your ideas so lovingly turned into columns, magazines and books.

Thanks to Marianne Garrow for all the support in the office, and speaking of the office, a huge THANK YOU to the person whose job it is to try and make sense of my diary: my executive assistant, Jeanette Curwood. She makes sure I get to the right places and on the right planes. It's no easy job, but we have worked successfully as a partnership over a long period of time now.

I've known Jeanette since my playing days at Richmond. She re-entered my life in the late 1990s to help me find the balance between coaching a modern football side and getting out and promoting the game. She probably deserved a premiership medal as much as anyone else in 2000.

And to everyone else to whom I have spoken, or listened, over 70 years of my life so far, thank you.

KEVIN SHEEDY

IMAGE CREDITS

Page 19 (top): Essendon FC
Page 19 (bottom): News Ltd / Newspix
Page 21: News Ltd / Newspix
Page 23: Richmond FC
Page 24: Richmond FC
Page 28 (top left and right): Richmond FC
Page 28 (bottom): News Ltd / Newspix
Page 31: News Ltd / Newspix
Page 32 (top and bottom): Richmond FC
Page 33: Richmond FC
Page 35: News Ltd / Newspix
Page 37: News Ltd / Newspix
Page 38: News Ltd / Newspix
Page 41: News Ltd / Newspix
Page 42: Richmond FC
Page 43: Richmond FC
Page 44: Richmond FC
Page 46: News Ltd / Newspix
Page 49: News Ltd / Newspix
Page 50: News Ltd / Newspix
Page 52–53: News Ltd / Newspix
Page 54: News Ltd / Newspix
Page 55 (top and bottom): News Ltd / Newspix
Page 56: Richmond FC
Page 57: Fairfax Media
Page 58: News Ltd / Newspix
Page 59 (top and bottom): Richmond FC
Page 62: News Ltd / Newspix
Page 65: Richmond FC
Page 66: Richmond FC
Page 68: Richmond FC
Page 69: Fairfax Media
Page 70: Craig Borrow / Newspix
Page 72–73: News Ltd / Newspix
Page 74: Essendon FC
Page 75: News Ltd / Newspix
Page 77: Essendon FC
Page 78–79: Richmond FC
Page 80: Essendon FC
Page 81: News Ltd / Newspix
Page 83: George Salpigtidis / Newspix
Page 85 (bottom): News Ltd / Newspix
Page 86: Essendon FC

Page 89 (top): Essendon FC
Page 89 (bottom): News Ltd / Newspix
Page 90–91: News Ltd / Newspix
Page 92–93: News Ltd / Newspix
Page 94: Fairfax Media
Page 95: Terry Phelan / Newspix
Page 96: Essendon FC
Page 98–99: News Ltd / Newspix
Page 100: Fairfax Media
Page 101 (top and bottom): News Ltd / Newspix
Page 102: News Ltd / Newspix
Page 104–105 (all): Essendon FC
Page 106: Craig Borrow / Newspix
Page 107: Essendon FC
Page 109: Darren Tindale / Newspix
Page 110: Essendon FC
Page 112: Craig Borrow / Newspix
Page 113 (top): Clive MacKinnon / Newspix
Page 113 (bottom): News Ltd / Newspix
Page 115: News Ltd / Newspix
Page 116: Essendon FC
Page 118: Essendon FC
Page 120: News Ltd / Newspix
Page 122: John Feder / Newspix
Page 123 (top and bottom): AFL Media Department
Page 124–125: News Ltd / Newspix
Page 126: Essendon FC
Page 127: Provided by Jane Clifton
Page 128–129: Essendon FC
Page 130–131: Stuart Hannagan
Page 132–133: News Ltd / Newspix
Page 135: Essendon FC
Page 137: Darrin Braybrook / Fairfax Media
Page 140: Essendon FC
Page 142–143 (all): Essendon FC
Page 145: Craig Hughes / Newspix
Page 146: News Ltd / Newspix
Page 147 (top and bottom): Essendon FC
Page 148–149: Mark Smith / Newspix
Page 151: George Salpigtidis / Newspix
Page 152 (top): John Feder / Newspix
Page 152 (bottom): Kelly Barnes / Newspix
Page 153: Karen Dodd / Newspix

Page 154: Michael Dodge / Newspix

Page 155 (top): Vince Caligiuri / Fairfax Media

Page 155 (bottom): Norm Oorloff / Newspix

Page 159: News Ltd / Newspix

Page 160–161: John Donegan / Fairfax Media

Page 162: Phil Hillyard / Newspix

Page 163 (top): Michael Dodge / Newspix

Page 163 (middle): Ben Swinnerton / Newspix

Page 163 (bottom): Tim Carrafa / Newspix

Page 164: Michael Dodge / Newspix

Page 166–167: Shannon Morris / Newspix

Page 168: Colleen Petch / Newspix

Page 170: News Ltd / Newspix

Page 171 (top): Essendon FC

Page 171 (bottom): AFL Media Department

Page 172–173: Essendon FC

Page 175 (top): Colleen Petch / Newspix

Page 175 (top inset): Provided by Mal Michaels

Page 175 (bottom): AFL Media Department

Page 176–177: Michael Dodge / Newspix

Page 177: Ian Currie / Newspix

Page 180: Essendon FC

Page 181: Craig Borrow / Newspix

Page 183 (top): Essendon FC

Page 183 (bottom): Peter Ward / Newspix

Page 184 (top): Essendon FC

Page 185: Vince Caligiuri / Fairfax Media

Page 187: Vince Caligiuri / Fairfax Media

Page 189: 'Shooting Star' Gavin Wanganeen
gavinwanganeenart.com.au

Page 190: AFL Media Department

Page 191: AFL Media Department

Page 192: AFL Media Department

Page 193: AFL Media Department

Page 194 (top and bottom): AFL Media Department

Page 195: AFL Media Department

Page 198: Gregg Porteous / Newspix

Page 200: Greater Western Sydney FC

Page 202–203: Mark Evans / Newspix

Page 204: Greater Western Sydney FC

Page 205 (top): Greater Western Sydney FC

Page 206 (top): Phil Hillyard / Newspix

Page 206 (bottom): Greater Western Sydney FC

Page 211: News Ltd / Newspix

Page 212–213: Greater Western Sydney FC

Page 214: Mark Kolbe / Getty Images

Page 216 (top): Greater Western Sydney FC

Page 216 (bottom): Greater Western Sydney FC

Page 218: AFL Media Department

Page 220: Essendon FC

Page 221: Essendon FC

Page 222–223: AFL Media Department

Page 224–225: Wayne Ludbey / Newspix

Page 226: News Ltd / Newspix

Page 229 (top): Greater Western Sydney FC

Page 229 (bottom): Greater Western Sydney FC

Page 230: AFL Media Department

Page 231: AFL Media Department

Page 232: Essendon FC

Page 237 (top): News Ltd / Newspix

Page 240 (middle left): David Geraghty / Newspix

Page 240 (bottom right): Alan Funnell / Newspix

Page 241 (bottom): Wayne Ludbey / Newspix

Page 247 (top): Victorian Sport Awards

Page 247 (bottom): Victorian Sport Awards

Page 248: Essendon FC

Page 249: Victorian Sport Awards

Page 254 (top): Immerse Photography

Page 254 (bottom): Aria Studios

Page 255: Ben Sierakowski Life Times
Photography

Page 261: Norm Oorloff / Newspix

Page 262: Michael Dodge / Newspix

Page 263: News Ltd / Newspix

Page 264: Essendon FC

Page 266 (top): AFL Media Department

Page 266 (bottom): AFL Media Department

Page 267: Geoff Naismith

All other images from Kevin Sheedy's personal collection.

All reasonable effort has been made to attribute copyright and credit. Any new information supplied will be included in subsequent editions.